A BIBLIOGRAPHY OF NEW TESTAMENT BIBLIOGRAPHIES

By the Author:
The Origin of 1 Corinthians

A Bibliography

of

NEW TESTAMENT

BIBLIOGRAPHIES

Compiled by

JOHN COOLIDGE HURD, Jr.

*Professor of New Testament, Episcopal Theological
Seminary of the Southwest
Austin, Texas*

1966 · THE SEABURY PRESS · NEW YORK

Copyright © 1966 by John Coolidge Hurd, Jr.
Library of Congress Catalog Card Number: 66-16653
533-SP-466-3
Printed in the United States of America

PREFACE

This collection is intended to facilitate the historical-critical study of the New Testament. It is the compiler's hope that this tool will enable the student to find in the shortest possible time the considerable help which the bibliographies of the New Testament literature afford. Only a portion of these aids can be listed under "Bibliography" by a library's catalogue; even when listed they can receive no comment or explanation. Hence the need for this collection.

The great national bibliographical tools which cover all fields are not listed, although they are indispensable. They are, however, described in the standard library handbooks, as well as by Niels H. Sonne, "An Evaluation of Book Buying Tools in Theology for the American, English, French and German Book Markets," Proceedings of the American Theological Library Association, 7 (1963), 70-87. Nor are bibliographies of manuscripts or editions of the New Testament included. Otherwise, the compiler has tried to list those bibliographies which will be useful to the student regardless of their manner of publication. Admission standards have not been entirely uniform, however. In areas not well covered by bibliographical tools, the standards have been lowered somewhat, and vice versa. Moreover, particularly with the subject bibliographies, the emphasis has been on the recent literature, on the theory that the student once put on the right scent can follow it back as far as he desires.

The compiler is acutely conscious of the inadequacies of this collection. He gratefully acknowledges the help provided by the American Association of Theological Schools through the award of a Faculty Fellowship for the year 1964/65, during which time much of the material was gathered. He acknowledges also the gracious help of the librarians and staffs of the Library of the Yale Divinity School, the Andover-Harvard Library, and the Library of the Union Theological Seminary, and especially of his colleague in New Testament, Mr. Harold H. Booher, Acting Librarian of the Episcopal Theological Seminary of the Southwest, 1965/66. He has received nothing but encouragement from Mr. Arthur R. Buckley, Editor of the Seabury Press. None of these bears responsibility for the limitations of this project; they are due to the compiler alone. Now that he has returned to his desk and has put his notes in order, he has become aware of many sources that he should have consulted. Since, however, even the expenditure of considerable additional time would fail to uncover the many useful bibliographies undoubtedly hidden in unexpected places, the material in hand is being published as a "progress report." The compiler invites and urges users to contribute additions and corrections, looking toward a second, enlarged edition.

John Coolidge Hurd, Jr.

February, 1966

CONTENTS

METHOD OF USE: A NOTE TO THE READER

Two comments might be helpful to students who are new to the study of the New Testament. In the first place, it would be well if such a student paused a moment before beginning to work. The subject bibliographies listed in section III, D, are initially attractive, but frequently are more general than the problem at hand. Thus the student should analyze his project from the point of view of the indexer. Some problems involve certain key words, so that section III, C, would be of especial use. Others focus on certain New Testament texts, so that the student should consult bibliographies which are indexed by Scripture texts. Still others are bound up with a particular book of the New Testament, or with a special period in the history of New Testament criticism, or with the work of an individual scholar or school of scholarship. The student will find appropriate sections for each of these approaches in the collection which follows. Second, the student would do well to work backward chronologically, beginning with the most recent tools. Once he strikes useful material, the earlier references will come easily and quickly.

Abbreviations for the names of journals follow the sensible system used by New Testament Abstracts. Enough of the name is given so that in most cases the reader can recognize the title immediately. If not, reference to NTAb or to any standard list of journals will resolve the difficulty. The dates in the left margin are to be read as follows: The time reference opposite the beginning of the bibliographical entry gives the approximate date for the close of the period covered by that bibliography. (Note: "cont." = continuing.) A line below this time reference means that the bibliography covers earlier years as well. A date below this line gives the approximate beginning for the period covered, if it appears that the author intended to begin at a particular point in time.

I. SELECTIVE BOOK LISTS

A. GENERAL NEW TESTAMENT STUDY

Cont.
——
1960
    Scholars' Choice: Significant Current Theological Literature from Abroad. Richmond, Va.: Library of the Union Theological Seminary. No. 1 = Dec., 1960 [?].
      Published twice yearly. A selective checklist of foreign books chosen by a panel of fifty European scholars. The July, 1965, number listed 17 NT titles.

1965
——
    Gottwald, Norman K. (ed.). Theological Bibliographies: Essential Books for a Minister's Library. ("The Andover Newton Quarterly," 4, 1 [Sept., 1963].) Pp. 138.
      More than 325 of these books concern the NT. The titles are very well selected, arranged, and annotated. About one tenth are starred as "fundamental." Purchasing information is also given. Cont., AndNewtQuart, 6, 4 (Mar., 1966), 70-84.

1964
——
    Kee, Howard Clark; Young, Franklin W.; and Froehlich, Karlfried. Understanding the New Testament (2d ed.; Englewood Cliffs, N.J.: Prentice-Hall, 1965), pp. 455-463.
      A classified and annotated bibliography in narrative form which discusses about 150 items.

1959
——
    Essential Books for a Pastor's Study: Basic and Recommended Works. Edited and published by the Faculty of the Union Theological Seminary, Richmond, Va. 3d ed., 1960. Pp. 71.
      On the average, about 30 years out of date.

1959
——
    Metzger, Bruce M. (ed.). A Bibliography of Bible Study for Theological Students. 2d ed. rev. Princeton, N.J.: Princeton Theological Seminary, 1960. Pp. 107.
      A classified list of some 1,300 books published through 1959. Includes conservative as well as critical works, with no attempt to distinguish between them.

1959
——
    Smith, Wilbur M. Treasury of Books for Bible Study. Natick, Mass.: W. A. Wilde Co., 1960. Pp. 288.
      The author is exceedingly conservative.

1959
——
    Crownfield, Frederic R. A Historical Approach to the New Testament (New York: Harper, 1960), pp. 389-403.
      A classified discussion of over 250 books.

1958
——
    Knox, John, and Beker, J. Christiaan (NT eds.). A Basic Bibliography for Ministers, Selected and Annotated by the Faculty of Union Theological Seminary, New York. 2d ed. New York: Union Theological Seminary Book Service, 1960. Pp. 139. [= UnSemQuartRev, 14, 2 (Jan., 1959), 51-57.]
      Eighty well-chosen books are listed in the NT area, 13 of which are starred as "essential."

1958
——
    Grant, Frederick C. "Selected Bibliography," in his preface to Johannes Weiss, Earliest Christianity ("Harper Torchbooks"; New York: Harper & Brothers, 1959), I, xiii-xxii.
      A classified listing of some 150 important books on the background of the NT, on the NT, and on early Christian history.

1955
——
    Grant, Frederick C. "Books for Further Reading," Chapter 11 of How to Read The Bible (New York: Morehouse-Gorham, 1956), pp. 157-168.
      An introductory list of books primarily intended for serious lay persons. Also some suggestions concerning tools for Bible study.

1955   Rowlingson, Donald T. Introduction to New Testament Study (New York: Macmillan,
——   1956), pp. 232-243.
        A classified bibliography of over 100 well-selected books with useful annotations.

1954   Essential Books for a Pastor's Library: Basic and Recommended Works. Selected, an-
——   notated, and published by the Faculty of the Union Theological Seminary, Richmond, Va.
        2d ed., 1955. Pp. 54.
        About 75 titles in the NT area, including a number of older, conservative works.

1951   Grant, Frederick C. (NT ed.). A Basic Theological Bibliography for Ministers, Selected
——   and Annotated by the Faculty of Union Theological Seminary, New York. New York: Union
        Theological Seminary Book Service, 1952. Pp. 57. [= UnSemQuartRev, 5, 2 (Jan., 1950),
        12-16, revised.]

1951   Graystone, G. "Bibliography [English and Roman Catholic] of Christ and the Gospels,"
——   Scripture, 5 (1952/53), 153-160; "Catholic [English] Bibliography of St. Paul's Life and
        Writings; of Acts, Catholic Epistles and Apocalypse," Scripture, 6 (1953/54), 56-59.

1947   A Bibliography of Bible Study for Theological Students. ("Princeton Seminary Pam-
——   phlets," No. 1.) Princeton, N.J.: Princeton Theological Seminary Library, 1948. Pp. 85.

1946   Hoskyns, Edwyn, and Davey, Noel. "A Bibliography," appendix B of The Riddle of the
——   New Testament (3d ed.; London: Faber & Faber, 1947), pp. 205-230.
        A classified list by areas of about 400 books mostly published before 1936. A special
        section (pp. 218-230) lists commentaries to the various NT books.

1945   Riddle, Donald W., and Hutson, Harold H. New Testament Life and Literature (Chicago,
——   Ill.: The University of Chicago Press, 1946), pp. 234-250.
        A classified bibliography of more than 300 well-selected books.

1945   Scammon, John H. (ed.). Theological Bibliographies. ("The Andover Newton Theolog-
——   ical School Bulletin," 38, 2 [Feb., 1946].) Pp. 32.
        Books recommended for a minister's library.

1945   Lattey, C. "Bibliography [English and Roman Catholic] of Christ and the Gospels,"
——   Scripture, 1 (1946), 38-41; Barton, John M. T. "Bibliography [English and Roman Cath-
        olic] of St. Paul's Life and Writings," Scripture, 1 (1946), 61-65; Theissen, A. "Catholic
        [English] Bibliography of Acts, Catholic Epistles and Apocalypse," Scripture, 2 (1947),
        53-57.

1940   Donovan, Winfred N., et al. (NT eds.). Theological Bibliographies. ("The Andover New-
——   ton Theological School Bulletin," 33, 3 [Apr., 1941].) Pp. 35.
        Books recommended for a minister's library.

1921   Frame, James E., et al. (eds.). "A List of Books on the New Testament," Bulletin of the
——   Union Theological Seminary, 5, 2 (Jan., 1922), 18-40.

1917   A Theological Bibliography. New York: Union Theological Seminary, 1918. Pp. 20.
——   [= "Union Theological Seminary Bulletin," 1, 4 (May, 1918), 58-75.]

1916   A Bibliography: Books for a Minister's Study. Chosen by the Faculty of the Yale School
——   of Religion. ("Yale Divinity Quarterly," 13, 4 [Mar., 1917], 214-249.)

1916   A Theological Bibliography for Ministers and Theological Students. ("Bulletin of the
——   Western Theological Seminary," 10, 1 [Oct., 1917].) Pp. 76.

1913   Theological Bibliographies. ("The Newton Theological Institution Bulletin," 6, 2 [Feb.,
——   1914].) Pp. 36.

1910   Votaw, Clyde Weber. Books for New Testament Study: Professional and Popular. 3d ed.
——   Chicago, Ill.: The University of Chicago Press, [1911]. [= The Biblical World, 37 (Jan.-
        Jun., 1911), 289-352.]
        About 850 titles briefly annotated. Topical arrangement. Periodicals list, pp. 349-352.
        Indexed.

1909   Theological Bibliographies. ("The Newton Theological Institution Bulletin," 2, 3 [Feb.,
———   1910].) Pp. 32.

1906   Schaff, Philip. Theological Propaedeutic: A General Introduction to the Study of Theol-
———   ogy:...A Manual for Students. 7th ed. New York: Charles Scribner's Sons, 1907. Pp.
        596.
           Numerous bibliographies included, among them one by Samuel M. Jackson, "A Minis-
        terial Library," pp. 537-596.

1904   Votaw, Clyde Weber. Books for New Testament Study: Popular and Professional. 2d ed.
———   Chicago, Ill.: The University of Chicago Press, 1905. [= The Biblical World, 26 (Jul.-
        Dec., 1905), 271-320.]
           A classified bibliography, briefly annotated.

1899   Votaw, Clyde Weber, and Bradley, Charles Fred. Books for New Testament Study: Pop-
———   ular and Professional. Chicago, Ill.: The University of Chicago Press, 1900. [= The
        Biblical World, 16 (Jul.-Dec., 1900), 42-80.]
           Works recommended by "The Council of Seventy," a representative group of Bible
        teachers. Classified. Not indexed.

B. SPECIAL TOOLS OF STUDY

1964   Swellengrebel, J. F. "Helps for Translators," Bulletin of the United Bible Societies, No.
———   62 (Apr.-Jun., 1965), 68-71.

1963   Martin, James P. "Theological Wordbooks: Tools for the Preacher," Interpretation, 18
———   (1964), 304-328. [= BibTrans, 16 (1965), 1-20.]

1962   Jones, D. R. "Aids to the Study of the Bible: A Selective Historical Account of the Major
———   Grammars, Lexicons, Concordances, Dictionaries and Encyclopaedias, and Atlases;
        Commentaries: A Historical Note," Appendices 1 and 2 to The Cambridge History of the
        Bible: The West from the Reformation to the Present Day, edited by S. L. Greenslade
        (Cambridge, Eng.: The University Press, 1963), pp. 520-535.

1962   Aldrich, Ella V., and Camp, Thomas E. Using Theological Books and Libraries. Engle-
———   wood Cliffs, N.J.: Prentice-Hall, 1963. Pp. 119.
           Not only a good explanation of the mechanics of using a library, but also a guide to the
        chief reference tools of a theological library. Ends with a chapter on how to make a
        bibliography.

1960   Glanzman, George S., and Fitzmyer, Joseph A. An Introductory Bibliography for the
———   Study of Scripture. ("Woodstock Papers: Occasional Essays for Theology" No. 5.)
        Westminster, Md.: Newman Press, 1961. Pp. 135.
           A classified and annotated list of 342 basic books for serious biblical study. Ex-
        tremely useful.

1959   Danker, Frederick W. Multipurpose Tools for Bible Study. St. Louis, Mo.: Concordia
———   Publishing House, 1960. Pp. 289.
           An interesting bibliographical discussion of the tools of Bible study. Very useful if
        allowance is made for the author's biblicistic point of view.

1958   Montgomery, John Warwick. The Writing of Research Papers in Theology: An Intro-
———   ductory Lecture—with a List of Basic Reference Tools for the Theological Student.
        Chicago, Ill.: University of Chicago Divinity School, 1959. Pp. 38.
           An excellent discussion of basic library tools.

1953   Smith, Wilbur M. A Bibliography of Biblical, Ecclesiastical and Theological Dictionaries
———   and Encyclopaedias Published in Great Britain and America. ("Fuller Library Bulletin,"
        Nos. 20-23 [Oct., 1953-Sept., 1954].) Pp. 30.
           A careful and exact alphabetical list compiled by a very conservative scholar. He
        omits tools which cover only the NT, since they do not treat the entire "Word of God."
        Works prior to 1850 are listed by title only.

1952   Barrett, C. K. "New Testament Commentaries: I. Classical Commentaries; II. Gos-
——   pels and Acts; III. Epistles and Revelation," ExpTimes, 65 (1953/54), 109-111, 143-146,
       177-180.
          A useful discussion of commentaries by series and by individual books.

1949   Kelly, Balmer H., and Miller, Donald G. (eds.). Tools for Bible Study. Richmond, Va.:
——   John Knox Press, 1956. Pp. 159.
          Composed of articles which appeared in Interpretation from 1947 to 1949 on NT lexi-
       cons, grammars, concordances, and commentaries.

1929   Clogg, F. B. "Recent Linguistic Aids to the Study of the New Testament," ExpTimes, 42
——   (1930/31), 463-464.

1926   Peake, Arthur S. "Commentaries on the Old and New Testaments," ExpTimes, 39
——   (1927/28), 245-249, 297-301, 361-365, 389-394.

1901   Bond, Henry. "The Best Bible Commentaries: New Testament," ExpTimes, 14 (1902),
——   203-205 (cf. pp. 358-359).

1892   Thayer, Joseph Henry. Books and Their Use: An Address, to Which is Appended [pp.
——   39-94] a List of Books for Students of the New Testament. Boston: Houghton Mifflin,
       1893. Pp. 94.

II. HISTORICAL AND CHRONOLOGICAL SURVEYS

A. HISTORICAL SURVEYS OF NEW TESTAMENT STUDY

1964   Hunter, A. M. "New Testament Survey 1939-1964," ExpTimes, 76 (1964/65), 15-20.

1939

1964   Neill, Stephen. "Theology 1939-1964," ExpTimes, 76 (1964/65), 21-25.

1939

1963   Edwards, George R. "Opportunity for Interdependence: The Present State of New Testament Interpretation," Interpretation, 18 (1964), 285-303.

1963   Funk, Robert W. "Creating an Opening: Biblical Criticism and the Theological Curriculum," Interpretation, 18 (1964), 385-406.

1962   Rowlingson, Donald T. The History of New Testament Research and Interpretation: A Bibliographical Outline. Revised ed. Boston: Boston University Book Store, 1963.

1962   Grant, Robert M. A Short History of the Interpretation of the Bible. A revised edition of The Bible in the Church. New York: Macmillan, 1963. Pp. 224.

1962   Greenslade, S. L. (ed.). The Cambridge History of the Bible: The West from the Reformation to the Present Day. Cambridge, Eng.: The University Press, 1963. Pp. 590. [Bibliography, pp. 536-549.]

1962   Gardner-Smith, Percival (ed.). The Roads Converge: A Contribution to the Question of Christian Reunion by Members of Jesus College, Cambridge. London: E. Arnold & Co., 1963. Pp. 253.

1962   Schweizer, Eduard. "Some Trends in European New Testament Research of Today," ChicTheolSemReg, 54, 2 (1963), 1-10.

1962   Pinomaa, L. (ed.). Finnish Theology Past and Present. ("Theologia Fennica," 7.) Helsinki: Finnish Theological Literature Society, 1963.
     Chapter 1, by E. Haapa, covers Finnish biblical studies in the 19th and 20th centuries. A selected bibliography of work done since 1959 is appended.

1961   Neill, Stephen. The Interpretation of the New Testament 1861-1961. ("The Firth Lectures," 1962.) London: Oxford University Press, 1964. Pp. 360.

1861

1961   Fuller, Reginald H. The New Testament in Current Study. New York: Charles Scribner's Sons, 1962. Pp. 147.

1961   Robinson, James M. "Basic Shifts in German Theology," Interpretation, 16 (1962), 76-97.

1960   Barton, John M. T. "Roman Catholic Biblical Scholarship 1939-1960," Theology, 63 (1960), 101-109.

1939

1959   Marty, Martin E. (ed.). New Directions in Biblical Thought. "Reflection Books." New York: Association Press, 1960. Pp. 128.
     Brief essays on the history of biblical interpretation by W. D. Davies, James M. Robinson, Cyril Blackman, and James D. Smart.

1959   Colwell, Ernest Cadman. "New Testament Scholarship in Prospect," JournBibRel, 28
———   (1960), 199-203.

1959   Corston, John B. "The New Testament Today," CanJournTheol, 6 (1960), 191-199.
———

1959   Hunt, Ignatius J. "Trends in Biblical Study," AmBenRev, 11 (1960), 280-301.
———

1959   Cadbury, Henry J. "New Testament Scholarship: Fifty Years in Retrospect,"
———   JournBibRel, 28 (1960), 194-198.
1909

1958   Baird, William R., Jr. "Current Trends in New Testament Study," JournRel, 39 (1959),
———   137-153.

1957   Kümmel, Werner Georg. Das Neue Testament: Geschichte der Erforschung seiner
———   Probleme. ("Orbis Academicus: Problemgeschichten der Wissenschaft in Dokumenten
und Darstellungen," Bd. III, 3.) Freiburg: K. Alber, 1958. Pp. 596.
     The most comprehensive history of the study of the NT. Bibliography of bibliographies,
pp. 559-560, and brief biographies of principal NT scholars, pp. 560-584.

1954   Barton, John M. T. "Roman Catholic Biblical Scholarship," Scripture, 7 (1955), 50-56.
———

1953   Kümmel, Werner Georg. "New Testament Research and Teaching in Present-day Ger-
———   many," NTStud, 1 (1954/55), 229-234.

1952   Bea, Augustin. "Der heutige Stand der Bibelwissenschaft," StimZeit, 79 (1953), 91-104.

1951   Howard, W. F. "Some Recent Foreign Books on the New Testament" [title varies],
———   LondQuartHolRev, V, 33 (1927), 114-116, annually (except 1941-1945) to VI, 21 (1952),
1926   134-137.

1950   Esking, Erik. Glaube und Geschichte in der theologischen Exegese Ernst Lohmeyers:
———   Zugleich ein Beitrag zur Geschichte der neutestamentlichen Interpretation. ("Acta
Seminarii Neotestamentici Upsaliensis," 18.) Lund: Gleerup, 1951. Pp. 267. [Bibli-
ography, pp. 243-263.]

1950   Filson, Floyd V. "The Study of the New Testament," in Protestant Thought in the Twen-
———   tieth Century, Whence and Whither?, edited by A. S. Nash (New York: Macmillan, 1951),
pp. 45-69. [Bibliography, pp. 68-69.]

1950   Abba, Raymond. "Recent Trends in Biblical Studies," ScotJournTheol, 4 (1951), 225-240.
———

1950   Howard, W. F. "A Survey of New Testament Studies during Half a Century—1901-50,"
———   LondQuartHolRev, VI, 21 (1952), 6-16.
1901

1950   Hunter, Archibald M. Interpreting the New Testament: 1900-1950. London: SCM Press,
———   1951. Pp. 144.
1900   A topical survey of NT study 1900-1950 (particularly of British scholarship).

1949   Dodd, C. H. "Thirty Years of New Testament Study: Inaugural Lecture as Visiting Pro-
———   fessor of Biblical Theology," UnSemQuartRev, 5, 4 (May, 1950), 5-12.
1920

1948   Higgins, A. J. B. "Some Recent Trends in Biblical Scholarship," The Congregational
———   Quarterly, 27 (1949), 122-133.

1946   Howard, Wilbert Francis. The Romance of New Testament Scholarship. ("Drew Lecture-
———   ship in Biography," 1947.) London: The Epworth Press, 1949. Pp. 164.
     A lively survey of the work of five groups of New Testament scholars important in the
history of modern NT study.

1946   De Zwaan, Johannes. "The Unity of Purpose in New Testament Studies," JournTheol-
——   Stud, 49 (1947/48), 129-136.
        A survey of NT study since the Reformation.

1946   Schubert, Paul. "Urgent Tasks for New Testament Research," in The Study of the Bible
——   Today and Tomorrow, ed. H. R. Willoughby (Chicago, Ill.: The University of Chicago
        Press, 1947), pp. 209-228.

1946   Cobb, James H. "Current Trends in Catholic Biblical Research," in The Study of the
——   Bible Today and Tomorrow, ed. H. R. Willoughby (Chicago, Ill.: The University of Chicago
        Press, 1947), pp. 116-128.

1945   Enslin, Morton S. "The Future of Biblical Studies," JournBibLit, 65 (1946), 1-12.
——

1944   Schubert, Paul. "New Testament Study and Theology," RelLife, 14 (1945), 556-571.
——

1942   Craig, Clarence T. "Biblical Theology and the Rise of Historicism," JournBibLit,
——   62 (1943), 281-294.

1940   Cadbury, Henry J. "The New Testament in the Next Generation," JournRel, 21 (1941),
——   412-420.

1940   Riddle, Donald W. "Fifty Years of New Testament Scholarship," JournBibRel, 10 (1942),
——   136-140, 183.
1891

1940   Parvis, Merrill M. "New Testament Criticism in the World-Wars Period," in The Study
——   of the Bible Today and Tomorrow, ed. H. R. Willoughby (Chicago, Ill.: The University of
1920   Chicago Press, 1947), pp. 52-73.

1937   Craig, Clarence T. "Current Trends in New Testament Study," JournBibLit, 57 (1938),
——   359-375.

1937   Cadbury, Henry J. "The Present State of New Testament Studies," in The Haverford
——   Symposium on Archaeology and the Bible, ed. Elihu Grant (New Haven: American Schools
        of Oriental Research, 1938), pp. 79-110.

1936   Jackson, C. "The Seminary Professor and New Testament Research," JournRel, 17
——   (1937), 183-194.

1935   Dodd, C. H. The Present Task in New Testament Studies. Cambridge, Eng.: The Univer-
——   sity Press, 1936. Pp. 41.

1930   Purdy, Alexander C. "Das Neue Testament in der amerikanischen Theologie,"
——   TheolRund, n. F. 3 (1931), 367-386.
1620

1929   Williams, N. P. "National Contributions to Biblical Science: X. Great Britain's Recent
——   Contribution to New Testament Study," ExpTimes, 42 (1930/31), 393-396.

1929   Easton, Burton Scott. "National Contributions to Biblical Science: VIII. America's Con-
——   tribution to New Testament Science," ExpTimes, 42 (1930/31), 265-269.

1929   Taylor, Vincent. "National Contributions to Biblical Science: VI. The Contribution of
——   France to New Testament Science," ExpTimes, 42 (1930/31), 76-81.

1928   Dibelius, Martin. "National Contributions to Biblical Science: V. The Contribution of
——   Germany to New Testament Science," ExpTimes, 41 (1929/30), 535-539; 42 (1930/31),
        39-43.

1928   Salvatorelli, Luigi. "From Locke to Reitzenstein: The Historical Investigation of the
——   Origins of Christianity," HarvTheolRev, 22 (1929), 263-369 [with an index of authors].
1695

1926   Dobschütz, Ernst von. Vom Auslegen des Neuen Testaments. 2. Aufl. Göttingen:
——   Vandenhoeck und Ruprecht, 1927. Pp. 64.

1921   Willoughby, Harold R. "The Next Step in New Testament Study," JournRel, 2 (1922),
———   159-178.

1920   Moffatt, James. The Approach to the New Testament. ("Hibbert Lectures," second
———   series.) London: Hodder and Stoughton, 1921. Pp. 240.
        Chapters 4-8 comprise a brief history of the rise of "the Historical Method."

1920   Turner, C. H. The Study of the New Testament, 1883 and 1920: An Inaugural Lecture
———   Delivered before the University of Oxford on October 22 and 29, 1920. Oxford: The
1883   Clarendon Press, 1920. Pp. 66.

1918   Moffatt, James. "Thirty Years of New Testament Criticism," ExpTimes, 31 (1919/20),
———   132-137.
1889

1917   Montgomery, James A. "Present Tasks of American Biblical Scholarship," JournBibLit,
———   37 (1918), 1-14.

1913   Jones, Maurice. The New Testament in the Twentieth Century: A Survey of Recent
———   Christological and Historical Criticism of the New Testament. London: Macmillan, 1914.
1900   Pp. 467. [Bibliographies, pp. 13, 36, 60, 87, 120, 162, 188-189, 227, 261, 294, 313, 358-
        359.]

1910   Feine, Paul. "Positive Theological Research in Germany: The New Testament," Exp-
———   Times, 23 (1911/12), 497-502.

1910   Vidler, Alec R. The Modernist Movement in the Roman Church: Its Origin and Outcome.
———   Cambridge, Eng.: The University Press, 1934. Pp. 286. [Bibliography, pp. 274-279.]
1890

1909   Conybeare, Frederick C. History of New Testament Criticism. "A History of the Sci-
———   ences." New York and London: G. P. Putnam's Sons, 1910. Pp. 192. [Bibliography, pp.
        185-188.]

1907   Weiss, Johannes. Die Aufgaben der neutestamentlichen Wissenschaft in der Gegenwart.
———   Göttingen: Vandenhoeck und Ruprecht, 1908. Pp. 56.

1905   Nash, Henry S. The History of the Higher Criticism of the New Testament: Being the
———   History of the Process Whereby the Word of God Has Won the Right to be Understood.
        ("New Testament Handbooks," ed. S. Mathews.) New ed. New York: Macmillan, 1906.
        Pp. 192.

1905   MacConnachie, John. "The Liberal Movement in Germany," ExpTimes, 18 (1906/07),
———   153-155, 219-221, 263-266.

1902   Bacon, Benjamin W. "Ultimate Problems of Biblical Science," JournBibLit, 22 (1903),
———   1-14.

1900   Elliot-Binns, L. E. English Thought 1860-1900: The Theological Aspect. London: Long-
———   mans, Green and Co., 1956. Pp. 388. [Biblical studies, pp. 116-191.]
1860

1899   Glover, W. B. Evangelical Nonconformists and Higher Criticism in the Nineteenth Cen-
———   tury. London: Independent Press, 1954. Pp. 296.
1800

1898   Bousset, Wilhelm. "Zur Methodologie der Wissenschaft vom neuen Testament,"
———   TheolRund, 2 (1899), 1-15.

B. SURVEYS OF A DECADE OR LESS

1965   Hunt, Ignatius J. "Recent Biblical Study, 1963-1965," AmBenRev, 16 (1965), 120-170.
———   Mainly Roman Catholic works.
1963

1964   Crespy, Georges. <u>Contemporary Theological Thought in France</u>. "Scholars' Choice:
——   Sixth Annual Bibliographical Lecture." Richmond, Va.: Library of the Union Theo-
          logical Seminary in Virginia, 1965.

1964   Barton, John M. T. "Notes on Recent Work: Holy Scripture," <u>ClerRev</u>, 50 (1965),
——   527-533.
1963

1964   North, R. "Scripture Trends in 1964," <u>AmEcclRev</u>, 152 (1965), 361-397.
              More than 200 items for OT and NT together.

1963   Arnaldrich, Louis. "L'Essor Actuel des Études Bibliques en Espagne: Réalisation et
——   Projects," <u>EphTheolLov</u>, 40 (1964), 5-18.

1963   Wingren, Gustaf. <u>The Main Lines of Development in Systematic Theology and Biblical</u>
——   <u>Interpretation in Scandinavia [1959-1963]</u>. "Scholars' Choice: Fifth Annual Bibliograph-
1959   ical Lecture." Richmond, Va.: Library of the Union Theological Seminary in Virginia,
          1964.

1963   Hunt, Ignatius J. "Recent Biblical Study, 1961-1963," <u>AmBenRev</u>, 14 (1963), 590-621.
——   Surveys about 100 books, the majority of them Roman Catholic.
1961

1962   Käsemann, Ernst. "Neutestamentlicher Sammelbericht II," in <u>Verkündigung und</u>
——   <u>Forschung: Theologischer Jahresbericht 1960/62</u> (München: Chr. Kaiser Verlag, 1963),
1960   pp. 78-94.

1962   Barton, John M. T. "Notes on Recent Work: Holy Scripture," <u>ClerRev</u>, 48 (1963),
——   714-721.
1961

1962   Porter, Calvin L. "The Study of the New Testament in 1962," <u>Encounter</u>, 24 (1963),
          217-230.

1961   "Bibliography: New Testament," <u>RevExp</u>, 59 (1962), 206-213.
——

1961   Schweizer, Eduard. <u>Recent Theological Literature in Switzerland</u>. "Scholars' Choice:
——   Third Annual Bibliographical Lecture." Richmond, Va.: Library of the Union Theological
          Seminary in Virginia, 1962.

1961   Hunt, Ignatius J. "Recent Biblical Study, 1960-61," <u>AmBenRev</u>, 12 (1961), 328-360.
——   Mainly Roman Catholic works.
1960

1960   Wolf, C. Umhau. "Recent Roman Catholic Bible Study and Translation," <u>JournBibRel</u>,
——   29 (1961), 280-289.

1960   Barton, John M. T. "Notes on Recent Work: Holy Scripture," <u>ClerRev</u>, 46 (1961), 364-
——   370, 738-746.
1955

1959   Käsemann, Ernst. "Neutestamentlicher Sammelbericht," in <u>Verkündigung und</u>
——   <u>Forschung: Theologischer Jahresbericht 1958/59</u> (München: Chr. Kaiser Verlag, 1960,
1958   1962), pp. 97-108.

1959   Gamble, Connolly C., Jr. "New Testament Literature, 1959," <u>Interpretation</u>, 14 (1960),
          333-348.

1958   Tilden, Elwyn E., Jr. "New Testament Literature, 1958," <u>Interpretation</u>, 13 (1959),
          195-205.

1957   Jacks, Clive Franklin. "Survey of Recent New Testament Literature," <u>UnSemQuartRev</u>,
——   13, 2 (Jan., 1958), 47-52.

1957   Hamilton, Neill Quinn. "Research Abstract: The New Testament (1956-1957),"
——   <u>JournBibRel</u>, 26 (1958), 235-241.
1956

1957 Edwards, George R. "New Testament Literature from Midsummer, 1956," Interpreta-
——   tion, 12 (1958), 221-241.
1956

1956 Tilden, Elwyn E., Jr. "New Testament Literature, 1955 and 1956 (to Midsummer),"
——   Interpretation, 11 (1957), 71-85.
1955

1955 Stendahl, Krister. "A Report on New Testament Studies 1953-55," HarvDivSchBull, 21
——   (1955/56), 61-80.
1953

1955 Käsemann, Ernst. "Hinweise auf neuere neutestamentliche Forschung," in Verkündigung
——   und Forschung: Theologischer Jahresbericht 1953/55 (München: Chr. Kaiser Verlag,
1953 1956), pp. 148-168.

1955 Bowman, John Wick. "Research Abstract: The New Testament (1954-1955)," JournBibRel,
——   24 (1956), 185-191.
1954

1955 Michel, Otto. "Neutestamentliche Forschung, Überblick 1955," Für Arbeit und Besinnung,
      9 (1955), 226-237.

1954 Barton, John M. T. "Notes on Recent Work: Holy Scripture," ClerRev, 40 (1955),
——   477-482.
1952

1954 Stamm, Raymond T. "New Testament Literature, 1954," Interpretation, 9 (1955), 200-
      212, 339-359; 10 (1956), 188-208, 429.

1953 Cadbury, Henry J. "Current Issues in New Testament Studies," HarvDivSchBull, 19
——   (1954), 49-64.

1953 Smith, William E. "Survey of New Testament Textbooks," JournBibRel, 22 (1954), 254-
——   256.

1953 Schlier, Heinrich. "Zur Exegese und Theologie des Neuen Testamentes [1945-1953],"
——   Die Welt der Bücher (Literarische Beihefte zu Herder-Korrespondenz), 1 (1954/55),
1945 57-65, 113-124.

1953 Collins, John J. "Bulletin of the New Testament," TheolStud, 15 (1954), 389-415.
——

1952

1953 Bowman, John Wick. "Research Abstract: The New Testament (1953)," JournBibRel,
      22 (1954), 193-200.

1953 Metzger, Bruce M. "New Testament Literature, 1953," Interpretation, 8 (1954), 218-232.

1952 Grant, Frederick C. "Survey of Recent Theological Literature: New Testament,"
——   UnSemQuartRev, 9, 1 (Nov., 1953), 21-24.

1952 Graystone, G. "Catholic English Bibliography of General Questions on the Scriptures,"
——   Scripture, 6 (1953/54), 84-94.

1952 Bowman, John Wick. "Research Abstract: The New Testament (1949-1952),"
——   JournBibRel, 20 (1952), 260-267.
1949

1952 Caird, George B. "Recent Articles on Biblical Interpretation (1951-1952)," Interpreta-
——   tion, 6 (1952), 458-466.
1951

1952 Barrett, C. K. "Chronicle: New Testament," JournTheolStud, n. s. 4 (1953), 311-320.

1952 Davies, Paul Ewing. "New Testament Literature, 1952," Interpretation, 7 (1953), 213-
      223.

1952   Fürst, Walter. "Das Neue Testament als Weisung für die Gegenwart: Neutestamentliche Einzeluntersuchungen des Jahres 1952," in Verkündigung und Forschung: Theologischer Jahresbericht 1951/52 (München: Chr. Kaiser Verlag, 1953/54), pp. 202-213.

1951   Käsemann, Ernst. "Probleme neutestamentlicher Arbeit in Deutschland," Beiträge zur
——   evangelischen Theologie, 15 (1952), 133-152.

1951   Barton, John M. T. "Notes on Recent Work: Holy Scripture," ClerRev, 37 (1952), 219-
——   299, 544-552.

1951   Collins, John J. "Bulletin of the New Testament," TheolStud, 13 (1952), 205-219.
——

1951   Quanbeck, Warren H. "Survey of Literature on the New Testament (1950-1951),"
——   Interpretation, 6 (1952), 230-237.
1950

1951   Barrett, C. K. "Chronicle: New Testament," JournTheolStud, n. s. 3 (1952), 312-320.

1950   Schmid, J. "Auslandsliteratur zum Neue Testament," TheolRev, 47 (1951), 81-100.

1950   Terrien, Samuel L. "Biblical Interpretation in Recent Periodicals (1948-1950),"
——   Interpretation, 5 (1951), 92-102.
1948

1950   Käsemann, Ernst. "Ein neutestamentlicher Überblick," in Verkündigung und Forschung:
——   Theologischer Jahresbericht 1949/50 (München: Chr. Kaiser Verlag, 1951/52), pp. 191-
1949   218.

1950   Barrett, C. K. "Chronicle: New Testament," JournTheolStud, n. s. 2 (1951), 245-256.

1949   Schweitzer, Wolfgang. "Annotated Bibliography on Biblical Interpretation," Interpretation,
——   4 (1950), 342-357.

1949   Lindeskog, Gösta. "Nordische Literatur zum Neuen Testament 1939-1949," TheolRund,
——   n. F. 18 (1950), 216-238, 288-317.
1939

1949   Berkemeyer, William C. "New Testament Literature, 1949," Interpretation, 4 (1950),
        202-211.

1949   Barrett, C. K. "Chronicle: New Testament," JournTheolStud, n. s. 1 (1950), 247-256.

1948   Grant, Frederick C. "A Survey of Recent Theological Literature: New Testament,"
——   UnSemQuartRev, 4, 4 (May, 1949), 27-32.

1948   Bartsch, Hans-Werner. Handbuch der evangelisch-theologischen Arbeit, 1938-1948.
——   Stuttgart: Evangel. Verlagswerk, 1949. Pp. 138. [On NT see pp. 44-78.]
1938

1948   Schweizer, Eduard. " 'Prophezei,' Eschatologie, Gemeinde: Überblick über die seit 1940
——   in der Schweiz erscheinene Literatur zum Neuen Testament," in Verkündigung und
1940   Forschung: Theologischer Jahresbericht 1947/48 (München: Chr. Kaiser Verlag, 1949/
        50), pp. 62-75.

1948   Craig, Clarence T. "Research Abstract: New Testament Research [1947-1948],"
——   JournBibRel, 17 (1949), 124-128.
1947

1948   Käsemann, Ernst. "Aus der neutestamentlichen Arbeit der letzten Jahre," in
——   Verkündigung und Forschung: Theologischer Jahresbericht 1947/48 (München: Chr.
1947   Kaiser Verlag, 1949/50), pp. 195-223.

1948   Tilden, Elwyn E., Jr. "New Testament Literature, 1948," Interpretation, 3 (1949),
        206-211.

1947   Grant, Frederick C. "A Survey of Recent Theological Literature: Current New Testa-
——   ment Books," UnSemQuartRev, 3, 2 (Jan., 1948), 23-27.

1947 Grant, Robert M. "Recent French Literature on the History of Interpretation,"
──── AnglTheolRev, 30 (1948), 57-60

1947 Grobel, Kendrick. "Amerikanische Literatur zum Neuen Testament seit 1938,"
──── TheolRund, n. F. 17 (1948), 142-156.
1938

1947 Metzger, Bruce M., and Piper, Otto A. "New Testament Literature, 1947," Interpreta-
      tion, 2 (1948), 218-233.

1947 Steinborn, Erwin. "Deutsche theologische Bücher des Jahres 1947," TheolLitZeit, 74
      (1949), 308-320, 375-384, 440-448, 507-512.

1946 Beardslee, John W., Jr. "New Testament Interpretation in Recent Periodicals,"
──── Interpretation, 1 (1947), 499-506.

1946 Craig, Clarence T.   "Continental New Testament Research Today," JournBibRel, 15
──── (1947), 232-233.

1946 Theissen, A. "Catholic English Bibliography of General Questions Bearing on Sacred
──── Scripture," Scripture, 2 (1947), 116-118; 3 (1948), 27-29, 59-61.

1946 Sløk, Johannes. "Dänische Theologie der Gegenwart: Neues Testament," TheolZeit,
──── 3 (1947), 244-249.

1946 Filson, Floyd V. "New Testament Literature, 1946," Interpretation, 1 (1947), 68-73.

1945 Steinborn, Erwin. "Englische theologische Bücher 1939-1945," TheolLitZeit, 73 (1948),
──── 313-320, 569-576; 74 (1949), 123-128, 183-192.
1939

1945 Steinborn, Erwin. "Schweizer theologische Bücher 1939-1945," TheolLitZeit, 74 (1949),
──── 566-576.
1939

1945 Nikolainen, Aimo T. "Finnische Theologie in den Kriegsjahren 1939-45," TheolZeit,
──── 2 (1946), 265-276.
1939

1944 Grant, Frederick C. "A Survey of Recent Theological Literature: The New Testament,"
──── UnSemQuartRev, 1, 1 (Nov., 1945), 29-31.

1942 Coppens, Joseph. "Chronique d'Exégèse 1939-1942," EphTheolLov, 19 (1942), 102-129.

1939

1941 Schelkle, Karl Hermann. "Zur neueren katholischen Exegese des Neuen Testaments,"
──── TheolRund, n. F. 14 (1942), 173-199.

1938 Gutbrod, Walter. "Aus der neueren englischen Literatur zum Neuen Testament,"
──── TheolRund, n. F. 11 (1939), 263-277; 12 (1940), 1-23, 73-84.
1929

1937 Andrews, Mary E. "Recent Books in the Field of the New Testament," JournBibRel,
──── 6 (1938), 38-39.

1907 Ropes, James H. "Survey of Recent Literature: The New Testament," HarvTheolRev,
──── 1 (1908), 381 ff.

III. COMPREHENSIVE (RESEARCH) BIBLIOGRAPHIES

A. WHOLE NEW TESTAMENT

1. Books (and Articles)

Cont.
—
1876
Theologische Literaturzeitung [with 1939 is added: Monatschrift für das gesamte Gebiet der Theologie und Religionswissenschaft, begründet von Emil Schürer und Adolf von Harnack]. Leipzig: J. C. Hinrichs, 1876—. Vol. 90 = 1965.

Through 1938, a biweekly; since then, a monthly. Not published Jan., 1945-June, 1947. Each issue contains a NT section which reviews the most important books of the month and appends a list of important journal articles. Also listed are new books, German dissertations, notes about prominent scholars, and, occasionally, their bibliographies.

Cont.
—
1902
Theologische Revue. In Verbindung mit der [katholisch-] theologischen Fakultät zu Münster...herausgegeben von Professor Dr. Franz Diekamp [and others]. Münster i. W.: Aschendorffschen Buchhandlung, 1902—. Vol. 61 = 1965.

A bimonthly Roman Catholic review in newspaper format of current theological literature. Bibliographical sections edited by R. Samulski give a classified listing of new books and journal articles. An average of about 90 items are listed each year.

Cont.
—
1907
Revue des Sciences Philosophiques et Théologiques. Publiée par les Professeurs aux Facultés de Philosophie et de Théologie O.P., Le Saulchoir, Etiolles. Paris: Librairie Philosophique J. Vrin, 1907—. Vol. 49 = 1965.

Not published 1915-1919. A quarterly which publishes each year or two a "Bulletin de théologie biblique: Nouveau Testament," a comprehensive discussion of work in the field.

Cont.
—
1910
Recherches de Science Religieuse. Publiée avec le concours du Centre National de la Recherche Scientifique. Paris, 1910—. Vol. 53 = 1965.

A quarterly which has published since its founding a section entitled "Bulletin Critique." Included in this section have been a notable series of bibliographical "bulletins" concerning the NT. Two principal series are the "Bulletin d'Histoire des Origines chrétiennes," written in earlier years by J. Lebreton and now continued by J. Daniélou, and the "Bulletin d'Exégèse du Nouveau Testament," written by various authors, depending on the special area surveyed. Contributors include X. Léon-Dufour, J. Duplacy, J. Huby, and F. Prat.

Cont.
—
1914
See also: L'Année philologique (1924—) and its predecessor, Dix Années de Bibliographie Classique (1914-1924), both listed in III, E, 1, below. See the entries under "Testamenta," "Testamentum novum," etc.

Cont.
—
1921
Revue des Sciences Religieuses. Publiée sous la direction des professeurs de la Faculté de théologie catholique, Université de Strasbourg. Strasbourg: F.-X. Le Roux, 1921—. Vol. 39 = 1965.

Not published 1941-1946. A quarterly which provides approximately annually a "Chronique du Nouveau Testament," usually a bibliographical discussion of a single phase of NT research. Authors of this section include E. Jacquier, L. Vaganay, J.-B. Cocon, and J. Schmitt.

Cont.
—
1920
Elenchus Bibliographicus Biblicus, published in Biblica. Rome: Pontifical Biblical Institute, 1920—. Vol. 46 = 1965.

Easily the best and most comprehensive bibliography of biblical studies since 1949, the year in which the present editor, Petrus Nober, assumed responsibility. The rather detailed classification scheme is displayed (in summary) at the end of each volume. The

Elenchus appears in quarterly fascicles, which annually form one cycle of the classification system. (Note, however, that vols. 30 [1949]-32 [1951] form the first cycle of P. Nober's regime.) Since 1960, annual supplements to this bibliography have appeared in the journal Verbum Domini, also published by the Pontifical Biblical Institute. Vol. 45 (1964) lists 4,197 numbered entries and the supplement adds another 792. Since reviews are not numbered, the bibliography probably includes 10,000 items. Not only books and journal articles are catalogued, but also dissertations, individual contributions to Festschriften, and book reviews. An index of authors (except authors of reviews), subjects (in Latin), and Scripture texts is given. Since 1958, Greek and Hebrew words have also been indexed. (For word studies prior to 1958, see the section "Philologia biblica.") The first time a book is listed, the author's name is printed in boldface type and the facts of publication are given. Then reviews are listed by reviewer's name and journal reference. In subsequent years the author's name may be listed again (this time in italics), together with the brief title of his book, in order that additional reviews may be listed. A cross reference indicates the initial entry for the book. The only drawback of this otherwise admirable tool (and of other comprehensive bibliographies published on an annual basis) is that most entries are about a year and a half old when they appear.

Cont.   Elenchus Bibliographicus, published in Ephemerides Theologicae Lovanienses. Louvain:
——   Universitas Catholica Lovaniensis, 1924—. Vol. 41 = 1965.
1924   This bibliography of books and articles covers the whole theological area, and is classified in broad categories. It appears in two semiannual parts which now have a separate pagination from the host periodical, EphTheolLov. Volume 40 runs to 341 pages of listings (about 8,000 items); about 850 items concern the NT. Indexed by authors. Note to librarians: The table of contents of the EphTheolLov is paged with the Elenchus, with which it has no connection.

Cont.   Quarterly Check-List of Biblical Studies: An International Index of Current Books, Mono-
——   graphs, Brochures and Separates. Darien, Conn.: The American Bibliographic Service,
1958   1958—. Vol. 8 = 1965.
           A list of books arranged alphabetically by authors with purchasing information. Only about 120 items are listed each quarter, and the time lag is rather great.

Cont.   Scripta Recenter Edita. Nijmegen, Holland: Bestel Centrale V. S. K. B., 1959—. Vol. 7
——   = 1965.
1959   Intends to give a complete listing of theological books published in the main Western languages. The emphasis is on speed, rather than on bibliographical details. Appears ten times a year. Indexed annually by authors and titles.

Cont.   New Titles in Theology and Related Fields. Berkeley, Cal.: Graduate Theological Union
——   Bibliographical Center. Vol. 1 = 1965.
1965   Published weekly since June, 1965. A mimeographed list of books grouped only by language in the theological area. Compiled from Bibliographie de Belgique, The British National Bibliography, Deutsche Bibliographie, Das Schweizer Buch, and Publishers' Weekly. Emphasis is on speed. Since it is almost unclassified, its main usefulness, other than to order-librarians, is to those who already know the names of the principal NT scholars and who want to check for recent titles.

1964   Kümmel, Werner Georg. Introduction to the New Testament. Founded by Paul Feine and
——   continued by Johannes Behm. Translated from the 14th German edition by A. J. Mattill, Jr. Nashville, Tenn.: Abingdon Press, 1966. Pp. 448.
           Easily the best NT "introduction" for English-speaking students. Excellent bibliographies appear at the beginning of each section. Indexed by Scripture texts, authors, and subjects.

1964   Robert, A., and Feuillet, A. (eds.). Introduction to the New Testament, translated by
——   P. W. Skehan, et al. New York: Desclée Company, 1965. Pp. 912.
           An elaborate product of French Roman Catholic scholarship. Numerous bibliographies are scattered throughout the text.

1962   Ward, A. Marcus, et al. A Theological Book List. Oxford: Basil Blackwell, 1963.
——   Pp. 202.
        Supplementary volume to R. P. Morris's below. Ward adds 1,046 English entries
(including many "evangelical," i.e., conservative, titles omitted from the 1960 list).
Also added are 1,442 French and 646 German entries. There are also Portuguese and
Spanish sections.

1959   The Shelf List of the Union Theological Seminary Library in New York City, in Clas-
——   sification Order. 10 vols. Boston: G. K. Hall & Co., 1960.
        A classified list of 203,000 books and pamphlets, giving by photographic reproduction
the catalogue card for each item. Few periodicals are included. There is no index. The
classification system and its rationale has been published by Julia Pettee, Classification
of the Library of the Union Theological Seminary in the City of New York, New York:
Union Theological Seminary, 1934 (with supplements). An exceedingly valuable tool.

1959   Morris, Raymond P. (ed.). A Theological Book List. Oxford: Blackwell, 1960. Pp. 242.
——   A comprehensive, classified bibliography of 5,472 books with annotations. More than
1,300 relate to the NT. The NT titles were selected by Paul Schubert, Paul Minear, Paul
Meyer, B. M. Metzger, V. Furnish, and Millar Burrows. Indexed by authors.

1957   Bibliographie Biblique. Montréal: Les Facultés de Théologie et de Philosophie de la
——   Compagnie de Jesus, 1958. Pp. 398.
1920   A classified bibliography of books by Roman Catholic authors and of articles from 29
Roman Catholic journals. Over 9,000 entries. The detailed classification system is
given in sequence at the front, and alphabetically at the back, of the volume. There is no
further indexing.

1956   Wikenhauser, Alfred. New Testament Introduction. Translated from the 2d German edi-
——   tion (1956) by Joseph Cunningham. New York: Herder and Herder, 1958. Pp. 580.
        An excellent reference "introduction" to the NT. Good bibliographies placed at the
head of each section. (For topics, see the table of contents.) See especially "The Most
Important Aids to the Study of the NT," pp. 10-17. Another fine Roman Catholic contribution to NT scholarship. Indexed by persons and subjects. More up-to-date bibliography will be found in the 3d (1959) and 4th (1961) German editions.

1950   Bowman, John Wick (ed.). Bibliography of New Testament Literature (1900-1950). San
——   Anselmo, Cal.: San Francisco Theological Seminary, 1953. Pp. 312.
1900   A mimeographed listing of 2,400 books and articles in English. Topically arranged
(see table of contents, pp. v-xii) with an index of authors. The articles are taken only
from ExpTimes, HarvTheolRev, Interpretation, JournBibLit, JournRel, and JournTheol-
Stud, and only for the period 1920-1950.

1946   Reicke, Bo. "Littérature exégétique acquise par les bibliothèques publiques de la Suède
——   1941-46." SvenskExÅrs, 14 (1949), 133-169.
1941   About 700 books on the OT and NT; international scope.

1945   Lyons, William Nelson, and Parvis, Merrill M. (eds.). New Testament Literature: An
——   Annotated Bibliography [1943-1945]. Chicago, Ill.: The University of Chicago Press,
1943   1948. Pp. 392.
        A comprehensive bibliography (3,432 numbered entries) which aimed at international
completeness. Most entries also contain an abstract or annotation. A large number of
reviews are listed under each book entry. Indexed by authors (but not by reviewers),
Greek words, and Scripture texts. Supplements and continues (in book form) Parvis,
1942, and Lyons, 1941 and 1940.

1944   Littérature Théologique et Ecclésiastique de la Suisse Protestante/Theologisch-kirch-
——   liches Schriftum der protestantischen Schweiz. Herausgegeben von der Kommission für
Literaturhilfe des Schweizer Evangelischen Kirchenbundes. Basel: Verlag Friedrich
Reinhart, 1945. Pp. 48.
        A bibliography of works in print at the time of compilation.

1944 Reicke, Bo. "Ouvrages de Science Biblique Publiés pendant les Années 1940-44,"
——   Symbolae Biblicae Upsalienses, 3 (1944), 18-38.
1940   About 400 books; international scope.

1942 Theologisches Literaturblatt. Leipzig: Dörffling und Franke, 1880-1942. 63 Bde.
——   Published biweekly in newspaper format. Book reviews, new book lists, and monthly
1880 surveys of theological periodicals. Conservative scholarship. Merged with TheolLitZeit
      in May, 1943.

1942 Bibliographisches Beiblatt der Theologischen Literaturzeitung, 1. [-22.] Jahrgang: Die
——   Theologische Literatur des Jahres 1921 [-1942]. Leipzig: J. C. Hinrichs, 1922 [-1943].
1921 22 Bde.
          A comprehensive classified bibliography covering the whole theological field. Indexed
      by authors. The final volume contains 226 pages.

1942 Theologische Blätter. Herausgegeben von Karl Ludwig Schmidt. Leipzig, 1922-1942.
——   21 Bde.
1922   A monthly newspaper which reviewed books and gave professional news and notes. No
      more published.

1942 Parvis, Merrill M. (ed.). New Testament Literature in 1942. Chicago, Ill.: New Test-
      ament Club of the University of Chicago, 1943. Pp. 107.
          A mimeographed bibliography of about 500 entries which continues the series previ-
      ously edited by Lyons (see Lyons, 1941 and 1940). Arranged alphabetically by subject
      headings. Most entries are annotated rather fully. Due to the war, no European work is
      included. Contains a list of "1942 reviews of 1941 books." Author index.

1941 Lyons, William Nelson (ed.). New Testament Literature in 1941. Chicago, Ill.: New
      Testament Club of the University of Chicago, 1942. Pp. 78.
          A continuation (and supplement) of Lyons, 1940. The number of journals indexed is in-
      creased to 97. Few European entries. Includes a list of "1941 reviews of 1940 books."
      No index.

1940 Reicke, Bo. "Bibelvetenskaplig bibliografi för åren 1935-1940," SvenskExÅrs, 7 (1942),
——   148-181; 8 (1943), 171-199.
1935   About 1,200 books on the OT and NT; international scope.

1940 Lyons, William Nelson (ed.). New Testament Literature in 1940. Chicago, Ill.: New
      Testament Club of the University of Chicago, 1941. Pp. 34.
          A mimeographed bibliography arranged alphabetically by subject headings. Intended to
      be "complete," although, because of the war, few European items were listed. Each
      entry gives either a brief abstract or annotation. Many of the comments are lively and
      disrespectful. Entries for books also contain lists of reviewers and reviews. No index.

1939 Johansson, Johan V. "Nordisk bibelvetenskaplig bibliografi för åren 1915-1939,"
——   SvenskExÅrs, 4 (1939), 177-198.
1915   About 400 Scandinavian books on the OT and NT.

1934 Beijer, Erik. "Bibelvetenskaplig bibliografi för åren 1930-34," SvenskExÅrs, 1 (1936),
——   135-177.
1930   About 800 books on the OT and NT; international scope.

1933 Muller, P. H. (ed.). Bibliografie betreffende den Bijbel, den Godsdienst, het Christelijk
——   Geloof, de Kerkgeschiedenis, enz. 1882-1933. Lochem: N. V. Uitgevers-Mij. "De
1882 Tijdstroom," 1935. Pp. 792.
          Dutch works only!

1926 Moffatt, James (ed.). The Expositor's Yearbook: A Survey of the Biblical and Theolog-
      ical Literature of 1926. London: Hodder and Stoughton, 1927. Pp. 316.

1925 Moffatt, James (ed.). The Expositor's Yearbook: A Survey of the Biblical and Theolog-
      ical Literature of 1925. London: Hodder and Stoughton, 1926. Pp. 311.

1924 Windisch, Hans. "Literature on the New Testament in Germany, Holland, and the Scan-
——   dinavian Countries, 1921-1924," HarvTheolRev, 19 (1926), 1-114.
1921

1922   Grant, Frederick C. "A New Testament Bibliography for 1918 to 1922 Inclusive,"
——   AnglTheolRev, 6 (1923/24), 309-319; 7 (1924/25), 40-54.
1918   A topical and annotated listing of books and articles. Intends to include all serious NT
studies in English published in this period, and as many of the Continental ones as
possible.

1920   Windisch, Hans. "Literature on the New Testament in Germany, Austria, Switzerland,
——   Holland, and the Scandinavian Countries, 1914-1920," HarvTheolRev, 15 (1922), 115-216.
1914

1917   Moffatt, James. An Introduction to the Literature of the New Testament. "International
——   Theological Library." 3d ed., revised. Edinburgh: T. & T. Clark, 1918. Pp. 659.
       The "Pfeiffer" of the NT. A large collection of older bibliographical material given,
unfortunately, in very compressed form. Must be used with the Library of Congress Catalogue or the Union Theological Seminary Library Shelf List to obtain the full bibliographical references. Indexed by some subjects, a few authors, and Scripture texts.

1917   Grant, Frederick C. "A New Testament Bibliography for 1914 to 1917 Inclusive,"
——   AnglTheolRev, 1 (1918/19), 58-91.
1914

1913   Theologischer Jahresbericht: 1. [-33.] Band enthaltend die Literatur des Jahres 1881
——   [-1913]. Leipzig: J. A. Barth [and elsewhere in other years], 1882 [-1915]. 33 Bde.
1881   H. Holtzmann edited the NT section in the early years; M. Brückner and R. Knopf, in
the final volume. Volume 32 (for 1912) reached 1,023 pages. Consists of reviews of
books and articles. International in scope. Indexed.

1912   Bibliographie der theologischen Litteratur für das Jahr 1900 [-1912]: Sonder-Abdruck
——   aus dem 20. [-32.] Bande des Theologischen Jahresberichtes. Berlin: C. A. Schwet-
1900   schke und Sohn, 1901 [-1916]. 13 Bde.
       A classified bibliography which comprehends the whole theological field. No indexes.
In its peak year (for 1907) it contained 623 pages.

1901   Muss-Arnolt, W. "Theological and Semitic Literature for the Year 1901: A Supplement
to the American Journal of Theology and the American Journal of Semitic Languages and
Literatures," AmJournTheol, 6, 2 (Apr., 1902), and AmJournSemLangLit, 18, 3 (Apr.,
1902), 1*-112*.
       A topical listing of about 6,000 books and journal articles.

1900   Muss-Arnolt, W. "Theological and Semitic Literature for the Year 1900: A Supplement to
the American Journal of Theology and the American Journal of Semitic Languages and
Literatures," AmJournTheol, 5, 2 (Apr., 1901), and AmJournSemLangLit, 17, 3 (Apr.,
1901), 1*-108*.
       A listing of about 6,000 books and articles.

1900   Bibliographie der Theologischen Rundschau, 1900. Herausgegeben von W. Leuken.
Tübingen und Leipzig: J. C. B. Mohr (Paul Siebeck), 1902. Pp. 142.
       A classified bibliography of the whole theological area. Issued in four fascicles with
numbers of TheolRund for 1902. Indexed only by topic headings.

1899   Muss-Arnolt, W. "Theological and Semitic Literature [1899]: A Bibliographical Supplement to the American Journal of Theology and the American Journal of Semitic Languages and Literatures," AmJournTheol, 4 (1900), and AmJournSemLangLit, 16 (1900),
1*-48*.
       A listing of about 3,000 books and articles.

1899   Muss-Arnolt, W. "Theological and Semitic Literature [1898-99]," AmJournTheol, 3
——   (1899), and AmJournSemLangLit, 15/16 (1899), 1*-96*.
1898   A listing of about 5,000 books and articles.

1898   Muss-Arnolt, W. "Theological and Semitic Literature [1897-98]," AmJournTheol, 2
——   (1898), and AmJournSemLangLit, 14/15 (1898), 1*-132*.
1897   A listing of about 4,000 books and articles.

28 Comprehensive (Research) Bibliographies

1897
——
1896
Muss-Arnolt, W. "Bibliography [1896-97]," AmJournTheol, 1 (1897), 271-288, 555-576, 858-882, 1130-1150.

1875
——
1866
Theologischer Jahresbericht. Wiesbaden: Julius Niedner, 1866-1875. 10 Bde.

A comprehensive classified bibliography which in Vol. 6 reached 800 pages. No more published.

2. Journal and Festschrift Articles Only

Cont.
——
1949
Index to Religious Periodical Literature: An Author and Subject Index to Periodical Literature, Including an Author Index of Book Reviews. American Theological Library Association. Vol. 1 = 1949/52; Vol. 2 = 1953/54; Vol. 3 = 1955/56; Vol. 4 = 1957/59; Vol. 5 = 1960/62. The 1963 annual volume has been published (1965).

The intention of the ATLA is to publish the Index in two-year cumulations, with an annual volume in the alternate years. Initially 30 journals were indexed; currently 100 are being surveyed. The first two volumes indexed the following journals of interest to NT students: AnglTheolRev, Biblica, CathBibQuart, Interpretation, JournBibRel, JournTheolStud, RevBib, RevHistPhilRel, StudTheol, and TheolRund. Vol. 3 added ExpTimes, HarvDivSchBull, JournBibLit, NTStud, NovTest, TheolZeit, UnSemQuartRev, ZeitNTWiss, and ZeitTheolKir. Vol. 6 added TheolLitZeit. Consult the headings and cross references under "Bible: New Testament."

Cont.
——
1950
Internationale Zeitschriftenschau für Bibelwissenschaft und Grenzgebiete: International Review of Biblical Studies. Dusseldorf: Patmos-Verlag. Vol. I = 1951/52.

Originally published semiannually, it now appears in annual volumes. The most complete collection of abstracts (usually in German) of periodical and Festschrift literature concerning the Bible. Currently lists more than 2,000 items annually from 400 journals. The arrangement is by topic, with a table of classification at the back of each volume. Contains an author index as well.

Cont.
——
1955
"Zeitschriften-Bibliographie," ZeitNTWiss, 48 (1957), 281-296, and twice annually thereafter. Edited since 1959 by U. Wickert.

A selected and classified listing of articles from 35 to 40 leading journals and recent Festschriften.

Cont.
——
1956
New Testament Abstracts: A Record of Current Periodical Literature. Weston, Mass.: Weston College of the Holy Spirit. Vol. I = 1956/57.

The most convenient tool of its kind for English-speaking students. Currently it abstracts the NT contents of about 300 journals. In addition, it abstracts book reviews, gives notes on recent books, and provides brief biographies of leading NT scholars. Arranged by broad categories. Indexed at the end of each volume (i.e., every third issue) by author's name (as author, as reviewer, or as subject) and by Scripture text. Modestly priced.

Cont.
——
1957
Religious and Theological Abstracts. Myerstown, Pa.: Theological Publications, Inc. Vol. 1, no. 1 = Mar., 1958.

A collection of abstracts of journal articles in the whole area of theology. Only 166 items relating to the NT were listed in 1964, as compared to 1,200 abstracts in NTAb. Indexed by author, subject, and Scripture text.

1961
——
Metzger, Bruce M. Index to Periodical Literature on Christ and the Gospels. ("New Testament Tools and Studies," 6.) Leiden: E. J. Brill, 1965. Pp. 652.

A comprehensive, classified index to literature on Christ and the Gospels in 160 journals from the first year of their publication through 1961. Indexed by authors.

1957
——
Metzger, Bruce M. Index to Periodical Literature on the Apostle Paul. ("New Testament Tools and Studies," 1.) Leiden: E. J. Brill, 1960. Pp. 183.

A comprehensive, classified index to the Pauline literature in 114 journals from the first year of their publication through 1957. Some accidental omissions. Indexed by authors.

1957 Benson, Alphonsus, et al. (eds.). "Survey of Periodicals," CathBibQuart, 12 (1950), 99-
———   106, 221-225, 346-355, 460-463; 13 (1951), 89-96, 209-212, 328-335, 444-446; 14 (1952),
1949 74-81, 151-190, 263-285, 359-375; 15 (1953), 65-86, 213-236, 344-363, 470-484; 16
      (1954), 52-55, 193-200, 330-342, 458-478; 17 (1955), 54-75, 486-501, 584-612; 18 (1956),
      54-76, 158-170, 286-313, 387-428; 19 (1957), 109-131, 244-261, 361-382, 494-526; 20
      (1958), 83-102, 230-246, 362-379, 518-552.
          This department began modestly by listing the contents of principal biblical journals.
      In 1952, however, it was considerably expanded, the arrangement became topical, and 876
      items were listed. The number of items has fluctuated, but reached a peak of 1,051 in
      1956. In 1958 the list of NT articles was abandoned in favor of NTAb (Vol. 1 = 1956/57).

1950 Metzger, Bruce M. Supplement to Index of Articles on the New Testament and the Early
———   Church Published in Festschriften. Philadelphia: Society of Biblical Literature, 1955.
          A supplement to the next item which contains additions to the earlier list and continues
      it through 1950.

1949 Metzger, Bruce M. Index of Articles on the New Testament and the Early Church Pub-
———   lished in Festschriften. Philadelphia: Society of Biblical Literature, 1951.
          A classified list of articles published down to 1950 in volumes honoring important
      scholars. These articles are often overlooked because heretofore they have been dif-
      ficult to find. Indexes 573 volumes yielding 2,100 items.

1899 Richardson, Ernest Cushing. Periodical Articles on Religion 1890-1899 (Author Index).
———   New York: Charles Scribner's Sons for the Hartford Seminary Press, 1911.
1890

1899 Richardson, Ernest Cushing. An Alphabetical Subject Index and Index Encyclopaedia to
———   Periodical Articles on Religion: 1890-1899. New York: Charles Scribner's Sons for the
1890 Hartford Seminary Press, 1907.
          In 1,168 pages of very fine type it surveys more than 1,300 periodicals and 175 ency-
      clopedias!

3. Dissertations

Cont. See the Theologische Literaturzeitung (III, A, 1, above), which has included a special sec-
———   tion listing typewritten dissertations annually since 1949 and at irregular intervals in
       earlier volumes.

Cont. See the Elenchus Bibliographicus Biblicus (III, A, 1, above), which lists dissertations
———   along with books and articles in its regular sequence.
1949

Cont. Index to American Doctoral Dissertations, in Dissertation Abstracts (Ann Arbor, Mich.:
———   University Microfilms, Inc.) as a 13th number in each annual volume from Vol. 16
1955   (1955/56) on. Compiled for the Association of Research Libraries.
          Lists all doctoral dissertations accepted in the U.S. and Canada year by year, whether
      or not the institution submits its dissertations to University Microfilms for reproduction.

1960 Catalogue of Doctoral Dissertations, Princeton Theological Seminary 1944-1960. Prince-
———   ton, N.J., 1962.
1944

1954 Doctoral Dissertations Accepted by American Universities 1933/34-1954/55. Compiled
———   for the National Research Council and the American Council of Learned Societies by the
1933 Association of Research Libraries. Edited by D. B. Gilchrist. New York: H. W. Wilson
      Company, 1934-1955. 22 vols.

1952 Doctoral Dissertations in the Field of Religion 1940-1952: Their Titles, Location, Fields,
———   and Short Précis of Contents. (Supplement to Vol. 18, The Review of Religion.) Published
1940 by Columbia University Press for the Council on Graduate Studies in Religion in coopera-
      tion with the National Council on Religion in Higher Education, 1954. Pp. 194.
          Lists 81 dissertations under the heading "Bible."

1950   A Bibliography of Post-Graduate Masters' Theses in Religion. Prepared by The Com-
——   mittee on a Master List of Research Studies in Religion. Edited by Niels H. Sonne. Pub-
       lished and distributed by the American Theological Library Association, 1951. Pp. 82.
           There are 295 theses in the NT area; 31 more concern the Bible as a whole. Addi-
       tional NT titles are found in the theology sections.

1950   Stendahl, Krister. "Neutestamentliche exegetische Dissertationen in Upsala 1937-1950,"
——   in Verkündigung und Forschung: Theologischer Jahresbericht 1951/52 (München: Chr.
1937   Kaiser Verlag, 1953/54), pp. 46-56.

1939   Palfrey, Thomas R. and Coleman, Henry E., Jr. Guide to Bibliographies of Theses,
——   United States and Canada. 2d ed. Chicago, Ill.: American Library Association, 1940.
       Pp. 54.

4. Book Reviews

Cont. See the Elenchus Bibliographicus Biblicus (III, A, 1, above) and the explanation given
——   above of the manner by which reviews are listed in this fine tool. Reviewers' names are
1949   not indexed.

Cont. See the Index to Religious Periodical Literature (III, A, 2, above), which contains a large
——   section at the back of each volume listing books alphabetically by author and appending
1949   their reviews as they appeared in the journals indexed by this tool. No index of
       reviewers.

Cont. See New Testament Abstracts (III, A, 2, above), which abstracts only major reviews, but
——   which does index the names of the authors of these reviews.
1956

1964   Book Reviews of the Month: An Index to Reviews Appearing in Selected Theological Jour-
——   nals. Fort Worth, Texas: The Fleming Library of the Southwestern Baptist Theological
1962   Seminary. Vol. 1 = Nov., 1962-Sept., 1963 (11 nos. only); publication ceased with 3, 9
       (Jun., 1965).
           Book titles are listed by the Dewey classification, together with their reviews as culled
       from about 75 journals. Indexed by book authors.

1945   See also the four bibliographies edited separately and jointly by W. N. Lyons and M. M.
——   Parvis (III, A, 1, above).
1940

B. INDIVIDUAL BOOKS OR SECTIONS OF THE NEW TESTAMENT

1956f For compressed bibliographies on the history of the exegesis of NT books see the arti-
——   cles on each book in Die Religion in Geschichte und Gegenwart (III, D, below).

1. Four Gospels

1956   Grant, Frederick C. "A Selected Bibliography," appended to The Gospels: Their Origin
——   and Growth (New York: Harper & Brothers, 1957), pp. 203-207.
           A classified list of about 200 books on the Gospels and Acts.

1937   Taylor, Vincent. "After Fifty Years: I. The Gospel and the Gospels," ExpTimes, 50
——   (1938/39), 8-12.
1888

1930   Dodd, C. H. "Present Tendencies in the Criticism of the Gospels," ExpTimes, 43
——   (1931/32), 246-251.

2. Synoptic Gospels

1964   McArthur, Harvey K. "Basic Issues: A Survey of Recent Gospel Research," Interpreta-
——   tion, 18 (1964), 39-55.

1961 Beare, Francis Wright. <u>The Earliest Records of Jesus: A Companion to the Synopsis of</u>
——   <u>the First Three Gospels by Albert Huck</u> (Oxford: Basil Blackwell, 1962), pp. 25-28.

1959 Evans, Owen E. "Synoptic Criticism since Streeter," <u>ExpTimes</u>, 72 (1960/61), 295-299.
——

1924

1958 Taylor, Vincent. "Modern Issues in Biblical Studies: Methods of Gospel Criticism,"
——   <u>ExpTimes</u>, 71 (1959/60), 68-72.

1955 Schmid, J. "Neue Synoptikerliteratur," <u>TheolRev</u>, 52 (1956), 49-62.
——

1941 Filson, Floyd V. "Significant Books on the Message of the Gospels," <u>JournBibRel</u>, 10
——   (1942), 93-97.

1929 Schniewind, Julius. "Zur Synoptiker-Exegese," <u>TheolRund</u>, n. F. 2 (1930), 129-189.
——

1912 Weiss, Johannes. "Die synoptischen Evangelien," <u>TheolRund</u>, 1 (1897/98), 288-297;
——   2 (1899), 140-152; 4 (1901), 148-161; 6 (1903), 199-211; 11 (1908), 92-105, 122-133;
      16 (1913), 183-196, 219-225.

1909 Lebreton, Jules. "Bulletin d'Exégèse du Nouveau Testament: Les Évangiles Synoptique,"
——   <u>RechSciRel</u>, 1 (1910), 500-512.

3. Matthew

1961 Lohmeyer, Ernst. <u>Das Evangelium des Matthäus</u> ("Kritisch-exegetischer Kommentar
——   über das Neue Testament," begründet von H. A. W. Meyer, Sonderband; ed. W. Schmauch;
      3. Aufl.; Göttingen: Vandenhoeck & Ruprecht, 1962), pp. 427-429 [?].

1961 Strecker, Georg. <u>Der Weg der Gerechtigkeit: Untersuchung zur Theologie des Matthäus</u>
——   ("Forschungen zur Religion und Literatur des Alten und Neuen Testaments," 82;
      Göttingen: Vandenhoeck & Ruprecht, 1962), pp. 243-250.

1959 Bornkamm, Günther; Barth, Gerhard; and Held, H. J. <u>Überlieferung und Auslegung im</u>
——   <u>Matthäusevangelium</u> ("Wissenschaftliche Monographien zum Alten und Neuen Testament,"
      No. 1; Neukirchen Kreis Moers: Neukirchener Verlag, 1960), pp. 289-294 [omitted from
      the English translation].

1959 Blair, Edward P. <u>Jesus in the Gospel of Matthew</u>. Nashville: Abingdon Press, 1960.
——

1957 Nepper-Christensen, Poul. <u>Das Matthäusevangelium, ein judenchristliches Evangelium?</u>
——   ("Acta theologica Danica," 1; Aarhus: Universitetsforlaget, 1958), pp. 212-222.

1953 Stendahl, Krister. <u>The School of St. Matthew and its Use of the Old Testament</u> ("Acta
——   Seminarii Neotestamentici Upsaliensis," 20; Lund: C. W. K. Gleerup, 1954), pp. 218-
      238.

1953 Ljungman, Henrik. <u>Das Gesetz Erfüllen: Matth. 5, 17 ff. und 3, 15 Untersucht</u> ("Lunds
——   Universitets Årsskrift," n. f., avd. 1, bd. 50, nr. 6; Lund: C. W. K. Gleerup, 1954), pp.
      127-133.

1908 Plummer, Alfred. <u>An Exegetical Commentary on the Gospel According to S. Matthew</u>
——   (London: E. Stock, 1909), pp. viii-xi (first paging).

1906 Allen, Willoughby C. <u>A Critical and Exegetical Commentary on the Gospel According to</u>
——   <u>S. Matthew</u> ("The International Critical Commentary"; New York: Charles Scribner's
      Sons, 1907), pp. lxxxix-xciv.

4. Mark

1958 Cranfield, C. E. B. <u>The Gospel According to Saint Mark</u> ("Cambridge Greek Testament
——   Commentary"; Cambridge, Eng.: The University Press, 1959), pp. ix-xv.

1954   Cartledge, Samuel A. "Studia Biblica, XXIX: The Gospel of Mark," Interpretation, 9
——   (1955), 198-199.

1951   Taylor, Vincent. The Gospel According to St. Mark (London: Macmillan & Co., 1952),
——   pp. xiii-xx, 9-25.

1928   Lagrange, Marie Joseph. Evangile selon Saint Marc (5th ed. rev.; Paris: Librairie
——   Lecoffre, 1929), pp. iv-xii.

1924   Rawlinson, A. E. J. St. Mark, with Introduction, Commentary and Additional Notes
——   ("Westminster Commentaries"; London: Methuen, 1925), pp. 1viii-1x.

5. Luke-Acts

1960   Barrett, Charles Kingsley. Luke the Historian in Recent Study. ("A. S. Peake Memorial
——   Lecture," No. 6.) London: Epworth Press, 1961. Pp. 76.

1960   Williams, C. S. C. "Luke-Acts in Recent Study," ExpTimes, 73 (1961/62), 133-136.
——

1958   Mattill, Andrew Jacob, Jr. Luke as Historian in Criticism Since 1840 (Ph.D. disserta-
——   tion, Vanderbilt Univ., 1959), pp. 470-634(!).
1840

1956   Conzelmann, Hans. The Theology of Saint Luke, translated by G. Buswell (London: Faber
——   and Faber, 1960), pp. 235-242.

6. Luke

1960   Grundmann, Walter. Das Evangelium nach Lukas ("Theologische Handkommentar zum
——   Neuen Testament," 3. Abt.; Berlin: Evangelische Verlagsanstalt, 1961), pp. 39-42.

1958   Rehkopf, Friedrich. Die lukanische Sonderquelle: ihr Umfang und Sprachgebrauch
——   ("Wissenschaftliche Untersuchungen zum Neuen Testament," 5; Tübingen: J. C. B.
       Mohr, 1959), pp. 100-104.

1956   Laurentin, René. Structure et Théologie de Luc I-II ("Études Bibliques"; Paris: J.
——   Gabalda, 1957), pp. 191-223.

1952   Price, James L., Jr. "Studia Biblica, XXII: The Gospel According to Luke," Interpre-
——   tation, 7 (1953), 210-212.

1944   Sahlin, Harald. Der Messias und das Gottesvolk: Studien zur protolukanischen Theologie
——   ("Acta Seminarii Neotestamentici Upsaliensis," 12; Uppsala: Almquist & Wiksells,
       1945), pp. 393-404.

1940   Wellhagen, Julius. "Engelsksprakig litteratur till Lukasskrifterna åren 1900-1940," in
——   Anden och riket: Lukas religiösa åskådning med särskild hänsyn till eskatologien ("Ny-
1900   testamentliga Avhandlingar," 1; Stockholm: Svenska kyrkans diakonistyrelses bokförlag,
       1941), pp. 146-175. [Further bibliography, pp. 132-140.]

1929   Creed, John Martin. The Gospel According to St. Luke: The Greek Text with Introduc-
——   tion, Notes, and Indices (London: Macmillan, 1930), pp. 1xxxvii-1xxxix.

1926   Lagrange, Marie Joseph. Evangile selon Saint Luc (4th ed.; Paris: Librairie Lecoffre,
——   1927), pp. iii-vii.

7. Johannine Literature

1958   Hunter, A. M. "Recent Trends in Johannine Studies," ExpTimes, 71 (1959/60), 164-167,
——   219-222.

1955   Stanley, David M. "Bulletin of the New Testament: The Johannine Literature," Theol-
——   Stud, 17 (1956), 516-531.

1928   Bauer, Walter. "Johannesevangelium und Johannesbriefe," TheolRund, n. F. 1 (1929),
——   135-160.

1911   Meyer, Arnold. "Johanneische Literatur," TheolRund, 5 (1902), 316-333, 497-507; 7
——   (1904), 473-484, 519-531; 13 (1910), 15-26, 63-75, 94-100, 151-162; 15 (1912), 239-249,
        278-293, 295-305.

1898   Meyer, Arnold. "Die Behandlung der johanneischen Frage im letzten Jahrzehnt,"
——   TheolRund, 2 (1899), 255-263, 295-305, 333-345.
1889

8. Gospel of John

1961   Smith, Dwight Moody, Jr. The Composition and Order of the Fourth Gospel: Bultmann's
——   Literary Theory ("Yale Publications in Religion," 10; New Haven: Yale University
        Press, 1965), pp. 251-255.

1957   Niewalda, Paul. Sakramentssymbolik im Johannesevangelium? Eine exegetisch-histo-
——   rische Studie (Limburg: Lahn-Verlag, 1958), pp. xi-xxvi.

1957   Menoud, Philippe-Henri. "Les Études johanniques de Bultmann à Barrett," in L'Évangile
——   de Jean: Études et Problèmes, par M.-É. Boismard, F.-M. Braun, et al. ("Recherches
1947   Bibliques," 3; Paris: Desclée de Brouwer, 1958), pp. 11-40.

1956   Haenchen, Ernst. "Aus der Literatur zum Johannesevangelium 1929-1956," TheolRund,
——   n. F. 23 (1955/56), 295-335.
1929

1955   Braun, F. M. "Où en est l'Étude du Quatrième Évangile?" EphTheolLov, 32 (1956),
——   535-546.

1953   Howard, Wilbert Francis. The Fourth Gospel in Recent Criticism and Interpretation.
——   4th edition revised by C. K. Barrett. London: Epworth, 1955. Pp. 327. [Bibliography,
1901   pp. 312-316.]

1951   Barackman, Paul F. "Studia Biblica, XVII: The Gospel According to John," Interpreta-
——   tion, 6 (1952), 76-78.

1949   Corell, Alf. Consummatum Est: Eschatology and Church in the Gospel of St. John,
——   translated from Swedish (London: S.P.C.K., 1958), pp. 213-237.

1948   Schmitt, Joseph. "Chronique d'Exégèse et de Théologie Biblique: Le Quatrième
——   Évangile," RevSciRel, 23 (1949), 78-96.

1948   Andrews, Mary E. "The Fourth Gospel Since 1940," JournBibRel, 17 (1949), 168-174.
——

1940

1947   Behm, Johannes. "Der gegenwärtige Stand der Erforschung des Johannesevangeliums,"
——   TheolLitZeit, 73 (1948), 21-30.

1946   Menoud, Philippe-Henri. L'Évangile de Jean d'après Recherches Récentes. 2d ed. rev.
——   ("Cahiers Théologiques de l'Actualité Protestante," 3.) Neuchâtel: Delachaux & Niestlé,
        1947. Pp. 91. [Bibliography, pp. 78-88.]

1940   Scammon, John H. "Studies in the Fourth Gospel, 1931-1940," AnglTheolRev, 23 (1941),
——   103-117.
1931

1908   Bousset, Wilhelm. "Ist das vierte Evangelium eine literarische Einheit?" TheolRund,
——   12 (1909), 1-12, 39-64.

1905   Meyer, Arnold. "Das Johannesevangelium," TheolRund, 9 (1906), 302-311, 340-359,
——   381-397.

1904   Bousset, Wilhelm. "Der Verfasser des Johannesevangeliums," TheolRund, 8 (1905),
——   225-244, 277-295.

9. Acts (see also §5 above)

1962 Guthrie, Donald. "Recent Literature on the Acts of the Apostles," VoxEvang, 2 (1963),
———   33-49.

1961 Dupont, Jacques. The Sources of Acts: The Present Position, trans. by K. Pond. London:
———   Darton, Longman & Todd, 1964. Pp. 180.

1961 Mattill, Andrew Jacob, Jr., and Mattill, Mary Bedford. A Classified Bibliography of Lit-
———   erature on the Acts of the Apostles. ("New Testament Tools and Studies," 7.) Leiden:
 200 E. J. Brill, 1966. Pp. 504.
      A comprehensive bibliography of 6,646 items: books, journal articles, Festschrift
      contributions, and dissertations (published and unpublished). Cf. A. J. Mattill's 1959
      bibliography in §5 above.

1960 Haenchen, Ernst. Die Apostelgeschichte ("Kritisch-exegetischer Kommentar über das
———   Neue Testament," begründet von H. A. W. Meyer; 3. Abt.; 13. Aufl.; Göttingen:
      Vandenhoeck & Ruprecht, 1961), pp. 10*-13*, 13-47, 657-666.

1959 Grässer, Erich. "Die Apostelgeschichte in der Forschung der Gegenwart," TheolRund,
———   n. F. 26 (1960), 93-167.

1956 Williams, C. S. C. A Commentary on the Acts of the Apostles ("Black's NT Commen-
———   taries"; London: A. & C. Black, 1957), pp. vii-xvi.

1954 Gärtner, Bertil. The Areopagus Speech and Natural Revelation, translated by C. H. King
———   ("Acta Seminarii Neotestamentici Upsaliensis," 21; Uppsala: C. W. K. Gleerup, 1955),
      pp. 253-272.

1951 Bruce, F. F. The Acts of the Apostles: The Greek Text with Introduction and Com-
———   mentary (2d ed.; London: Tyndale Press, 1952), pp. ix-xiv, 49-55.

1950 Gettys, Joseph M. "Studia Biblica, XIV: The Book of Acts," Interpretation, 5 (1951),
———   228-230.

1950 Dupont, Jacques. Les Problèmes du Livre des Actes d'après les Travaux Récents.
———   ("Analecta Lovaniensia Biblica et Orientlia," Ser. 2, fasc. 17.) Louvain: Publications
1940 Universitaires de Louvain, 1950.

1925 Jacquier, Eugène. Les Actes des Apôtres ("Études Bibliques"; 2d ed.; Paris:
———   Librairie Lecoffre, 1926), pp. iii-xiv.

1922 Prat, Ferdinand. "Bulletin d'Exégèse du Nouveau Testament: Travaux Récents sur les
———   'Actes des Apôtres.'" RechSciRel, 13 (1923), 366-381.

1921 Foakes-Jackson, F. J., and Lake, Kirsopp (eds.). The Beginnings of Christianity, Vol. II:
———   Prolegomena, II: Criticism. London: Macmillan, 1922. Pp. 539.
      The whole volume is a history of various aspects of the criticism of Acts.

1920 Wikenhauser, Alfred. Die Apostelgeschichte und ihr Geschichtswert ("Neutestamentliche
———   Abhandlungen," VIII, 3/5; Münster i. W.: Aschendorff, 1921), pp. ix-xviii.

1916 Bauer, Walter. "Apostelgeschichte und apostolisches Zeitalter," TheolRund, 14 (1911),
———   269-294; 17 (1914), 209-223; 20 (1917), 115-138.

1912 Prat, Ferdinand. "Bulletin d'Exégèse du Nouveau Testament: Les Sources des Actes des
———   Apôtres," RechSciRel, 4 (1913), 275-296.

1907 Bousset, Wilhelm. "Neueste Forschungen zur Apostelgeschichte," TheolRund, 11 (1908),
———   185-205.

1903 Clemen, Carl. "Apostelgeschichte und apostolisches Zeitalter," TheolRund, 1 (1897/98),
———   371-377; 3 (1900), 50-56; 4 (1901), 66-79; 6 (1903), 79-90; 7 (1904), 278-286.

1898 Heitmüller, W. "Die Quellenfrage in der Apostelgeschichte (1886-1898)," TheolRund, 2
———   (1899), 47-59, 83-95, 127-140.
1886

10. Pauline Corpus

1963   Harrison, P. N. Paulines and Pastorals. London: Villiers Publications, Ltd., 1964.
——   Pp. 142.

1961   Rigaux, Béda. Saint Paul et ses Lettres: État de la Question. ("Studia Neotestamentica,"
——   Subsidia 2.) Paris: Desclée de Brouwer, 1962. Pp. 229.
            Detailed bibliographical survey of the introductory problems of the Pauline letters, the
        Pastoral Epistles, and Hebrews. Table of contents at back. Index of scholars.

1960   Guthrie, Donald. New Testament Introduction: The Pauline Epistles (London: Tyndale
——   Press, 1961), pp. 295-309.
            Includes the Pastoral Epistles.

1955   Collins, John J. "Bulletin of the New Testament: The Pauline Epistles," TheolStud, 17
——   (1956), 531-548.

1933   Duncan, George S. "Some Outstanding New Testament Problems: VI. The Epistles of
——   the Imprisonment in Recent Discussion," ExpTimes, 46 (1934/35), 293-298.

1916   Knopf, Rudolf. "Paulinische Briefe, II (Gefangenschafts- und Pastoralbriefe),"
——   TheolRund, 9 (1906), 62-65; 16 (1913), 22-32; 20 (1917), 239-247.

1903   Schmiedel, Paul W. "Paulinische Briefe, I (Rö. Kor. Gal. Thess.)," TheolRund, 1
——   (1897/98), 142-150; 4 (1901), 498-522; 7 (1904), 21-28, 62-75.

11. Romans

1962   Michel, Otto. Der Brief an die Römer ("Kritisch-exegetischer Kommentar über das
——   Neue Testament," begründet von H. A. W. Meyer; 4. Abt.; 12. Aufl.; Göttingen:
        Vandenhoeck & Ruprecht, 1963), pp. ix-xiv.

1960   Rhys, J. Howard. The Epistle to the Romans (New York: Macmillan, 1961), pp. 240-243.
——

1958   Rabanos, R. "Boletin Bibliografico de la Carta a los Romanos," Salmanticensis, 6
——   (1959), 705-790.
            A classified and annotated bibliography of 968 books and articles.

1956   Leenhardt, Franz J. The Epistle to the Romans: A Commentary, translated by H. Knight
——   (London: Lutterworth, 1961), pp. 29-30.

1950   Bonnard, Pierre. "Où en est l'interprétation de l'Épître aux Romains?" RevThéolPhil,
——   84 (1951), 225-243.

1929   Lagrange, Marie Joseph. Saint Paul: Épître aux Romains ("Études Bibliques"; Paris:
——   Librairie Lecoffre, 1950), pp. vii-xiv, 395-396.

1928   Schumacher, Rudolf. Die Beiden letzten Kapitel des Römerbriefes: Ein Beitrag zu ihrer
——   Geschichte und Erklärung ("Neutestamentliche Abhandlungen," 14. Bd., 4. Hft.; Münster
        i. W.: Aschendorff, 1929), pp. v-xi.

12. I Corinthians

1964   Hurd, John C., Jr. The Origin of 1 Corinthians (London: S.P.C.K., and New York: Seabury
——   Press, 1965), pp. 306-334.

1954   Vischer, Lukas. Die Auslegungsgeschichte von I. Kor. 6, 1-11; Rechtsverzicht und
——   Schlichtung. ("Beiträge zur Geschichte der neutestamentlichen Exegese," 1) Tübingen:
        J. C. B. Mohr, 1955. Pp. 139.

1952   Melconian, V. D. "Studia Biblica, XXI: First Corinthians," Interpretation, 7 (1953),
——   75-77.

1934   Allo, Ernest-Bernard. Saint Paul: Première Épître aux Corinthiens ("Études Bibliques";
────   Paris: Librairie Lecoffre, 1935 [= 1956]), pp. cv-cxii.

1911   Robertson, Archibald, and Plummer, Alfred. A Critical and Exegetical Commentary on
────   the First Epistle of St Paul to the Corinthians ("The International Critical Commentary";
       2d ed.; Edinburgh: T. & T. Clark, 1914), pp. lxvi-lxx.

13. II Corinthians

1936   Allo, Ernest-Bernard. Saint Paul: Seconde Épître aux Corinthiens ("Études Bibliques";
────   Paris: Librairie Lecoffre, 1937 [= 1956]), pp. lxxi-lxxv.

1914   Plummer, Alfred. A Critical and Exegetical Commentary on the Second Epistle of St Paul
────   to the Corinthians ("The International Critical Commentary"; Edinburgh: T. & T. Clark,
       1915), pp. lv-lviii.

14. Galatians

1961   Schlier, Heinrich. Der Brief an die Galater ("Kritisch-exegetischer Kommentar über
────   das Neue Testament," begründet von H. A. W. Meyer; 7. Abt.; 12. Aufl.; Göttingen: Vanden-
       hoeck & Ruprecht, 1962), pp. 9*-14*.

1959   Ramsey, Howard Lyn. The Place of Galatians in the Career of Paul (Columbia University,
────   Ph.D. dissertation; Ann Arbor, Mich.: University Microfilms, 1961), pp. 353-363.

1920   Burton, Ernest De Witt. A Critical and Exegetical Commentary on the Epistle to the Gala-
────   tians ("The International Critical Commentary"; Edinburgh: T. & T. Clark, 1921), pp.
       lxxxii-lxxxix.

15. Ephesians

1961   Schlier, Heinrich. Der Brief an die Epheser: Ein Kommentar (3. Aufl.; Düsseldorf:
────   Patmos-Verlag, 1962), pp. 8-13 [books only].

1953   Bowman, John Wick. "Studia Biblica, XXV: The Epistle to the Ephesians," Interpretation,
────   8 (1954), 204-205.

16. Philippians

1963   Schmauch, Werner. Beiheft to Die Briefe an die Philipper, an die Kolosser und an Phile-
────   mon. ("Kritisch-exegetischer Kommentar über das Neue Testament," begründet von
1928   H. A. W. Meyer, 9. Abt.) Göttingen: Vandenhoeck & Ruprecht, 1964. [Over 200 numbered
       items in bibliographies at the heads of the main sections.]

1958   Beare, F. W. A Commentary on the Epistle to the Philippians ("Black's NT Commen-
────   taries"; London: A. & C. Black, 1959), pp. 37-46.

17. Colossians and Philemon

1963   See Schmauch, § 16 above.
────

1928

1956   Moule, C. F. D. The Epistles of Paul the Apostle to the Colossians and to Philemon
────   ("Cambridge Greek Testament Commentary"; Cambridge, Eng.: The University Press,
       1957), pp. ix-xiii.

18. I and II Thessalonians

1955 Rigaux, Béda. Saint Paul: Les Épîtres aux Thessaloniciens ("Études Bibliques"; Paris:
——— J. Gabalda, 1956), pp. xv-xxxii.

1911 Frame, James Everett. A Critical and Exegetical Commentary on the Epistles of St Paul
——— to the Thessalonians ("The International Critical Commentary"; Edinburgh: T. & T.
Clark, 1912), pp. 59-65.

1907 Milligan, George. St Paul's Epistles to the Thessalonians: The Greek Text with Intro-
——— duction and Notes (London: Macmillan, 1908), pp. cii-cix.

1893 Bornemann, Wilhelm. "Zur Geschichte der Auslegung der beiden Thessalonicherbriefe,"
——— in his Die Thessalonicherbriefe ("Kritisch-exegetischer Kommentar über das Neue
Testament," begründet von H. A. W. Meyer, 10. Abt.; 5. u. 6. Aufl.; Göttingen: Vandenhoeck & Ruprecht, 1894), pp. 538-708. [See also the bibliography, pp. 1-7.]

19. Pastoral Epistles (see also §10 above)

1964 Moule, C. F. D. "The Problem of the Pastoral Epistles: A Reappraisal" ["The Manson
——— Memorial Lecture," University of Manchester, Oct. 30, 1964], BullJohnRylLib, 47 (1965),
430-452.

1962 Kelly, J. N. D. A Commentary on the Pastoral Epistles: I Timothy, II Timothy, Titus
——— ("Black's NT Commentaries"; London: A. & C. Black, 1963), pp. 37-38.

1959 Warren, M. A. C. "Commentaries on the Pastoral Epistles," Theology, 63 (1960), 15-19.

1946 Spicq, C. Saint Paul: Les Épîtres Pastorales ("Études Bibliques"; Paris: Librairie
——— Lecoffre, 1947), pp. iii-xix.

1920 Harrison, P. N. The Problem of the Pastoral Epistles (London: Oxford University Press,
——— 1921), pp. 179-184.

20. Hebrews (see also §21 below)

1964 Sowers, Sidney G. The Hermeneutics of Philo and Hebrews: A Comparison of the Inter-
——— pretation of the Old Testament in Philo Judaeus and the Epistle to the Hebrews. ("Basel
Studies in Theology," 1; Zürich: EVZ-Verlag, 1965), pp. 141-146.

1963 Grässer, Erich. "Der Hebräerbrief 1938-1963," TheolRund, 30 (1964/65), 138-236.
———
1938

1962 Spicq, C., in Supplément to the Dictionnaire de la Bible, publié sous la direction de L.
——— Pirot (Paris: Librairie Letouzey, 1928—), VII (1963), 272-279.
1952

1961 See Rigaux, §10 above.
———
1951 Spicq, C. L'Épître aux Hébreux: Vol. I., Introduction ("Études Bibliques"; Paris: Li-
——— brairie Lecoffre, 1952), pp. 379-411.

1951 See Guthrie, §21 below.
———
1938 Käsemann, Ernst. Das wandernde Gottesvolk: Eine Untersuchung zum Hebräerbrief.
——— ("Forschungen zur Religion und Literatur des Alten und Neuen Testaments," n. F. 37.
Hft.) Göttingen: Vandenhoeck & Ruprecht, 1939. Pp. 156.

1909 Burggaller, E. "Neue Untersuchungen zum Hebräerbrief," TheolRund, 13 (1910), 369-
——— 381, 409-417.

21. Catholic Epistles

1951   Guthrie, Donald. New Testament Introduction: The General Epistles and Revelation.
——   London: Tyndale Press, 1962. Pp. 320.

1914   Bauer, Walter, "Die katholischen Briefe (und der Hebräerbrief)," TheolRund, 16 (1913),
——   48-58; 18 (1915), 292-300.

1904   Kühl, E. "(Hebräerbrief und) Katholische Briefe," TheolRund, 1 (1897/98), 590-593; 4
——   (1901), 12-18; 8 (1905), 296-301.

22. James

1909   Mayor, Joseph B. The Epistle of St. James: The Greek Text with Introduction, Notes and
——   Comments. 3d ed. London: Macmillan, 1910. Pp. ccxx + 248.

23. I Peter

1957   Beare, Francis Wright. The First Epistle of Peter (2d ed. rev.; Oxford: Basil Blackwell,
——   1958), pp. 43-45, 186-188. [For a history of criticism 1946-1957, see pp. 188-204.]

1953   Love, Julian Price. "Studia Biblica, XXIV: The First Epistle of Peter," Interpretation,
——   8 (1954), 86-87.

1945   Reicke, Bo Ivar. The Disobedient Spirits and Christian Baptism: A Study of 1 Pet. iii.19
——   and its Context ("Acta Seminarii Neotestamentici Upsaliensis, 13"; København: E.
        Munksgaard, 1946), pp. 249-269.

24. Johannine Epistles (see also §7 above)

1959   Haenchen, Ernst. "Neuere Literatur zu den Johannesbriefen," TheolRund, n. F. 26
——   (1960), 1-43, 267-291.

1952   Schnackenburg, Rudolf. Die Johannesbriefe ("Herders theologischer Kommentar zum
——   Neuen Testament," Bd. 13, Faszikel 3; Freiburg: Herder, 1953), pp. xi-xviii.

25. Revelation (see also §7 above)

1962   Feuillet, André. L'Apocalypse: Etat de la Question. ("Studia Neotestamentica," Sub-
——   sidia 3.) Paris: Desclée de Brouwer, 1963. Pp. 122.

1951   See Guthrie, § 21 above.
——

1934   Lohmeyer, Ernst. "Die Offenbarung des Johannes 1920-1934," TheolRund, n. F. 6 (1934),
——   269-314; 7 (1935), 28-62.
1920

1932   Allo, Ernest-Bernard. Saint Jean: L'Apocalypse (3d éd. augm.; "Études Bibliques";
——   Paris: Librairie Lecoffre, 1933), pp. ccxci-ccxciv [history of interpretation, pp. ccxxxv-
        cclxxiv].

1914   Meyer, Arnold. "Die Offenbarung Johannis," TheolRund, 1 (1897/98), 47-62, 91-101;
——   10 (1907), 126-142, 182-187; 18 (1915), 199-207.

1912   Charles, Robert Henry. "History of the Interpretation of the Apocalypse," in his
——   Studies in the Apocalypse, Being Lectures Delivered Before the University of London
        (Edinburgh: T. & T. Clark, 1913), pp. 1-78.

1905   Bousset, Wilhelm. Die Offenbarung Johannis ("Kritisch-exegetischer Kommentar über
——   das Neue Testament," begründet von H. A. W. Meyer, 16. Abt.; 5. Aufl.; Göttingen:

Vandenhoeck & Ruprecht, 1906), pp. 48-118 [a history of interpretation; in the 4. Aufl. (1896), pp. 51-171].

C. NEW TESTAMENT WORDS

Cont. —— 1920   See the <u>Elenchus Bibliographicus Biblicus</u> (III, A, 1, above) and the explanation given there of the manner of listing word studies.

Cont. —— 1949   See the <u>Index to Religious Periodical Literature</u> (III, A, 2, above) under the heading, "Greek Language: Terms and Phrases."

Cont. —— 1950   See the <u>Internationale Zeitschriftenschau</u> (III, A, 2, above) under the heading "Sprache: Griechisch" in the main classification scheme.

1957   See Metzger, <u>Index to ... Paul</u> (III, A, 2, above), nos. 524-598 with cross references.

1957 ——   Bauer, Walter. <u>Griechisch-Deutsches Wörterbuch zu den Schriften des Neuen Testaments und der übrigen urchristlichen Literatur.</u> 5., verbesserte und stark vermehrte Auflage. Berlin: Alfred Töpelmann, 1958. Pp. [890].
A mine of bibliographical information. See especially the ends of the individual articles.

1954 ——   Arndt, William F., and Gingrich, F. Wilbur. <u>A Greek-English Lexicon of the New Testament and Other Early Christian Literature: A translation and adaptation of Walter Bauer's Griechisch-Deutsches Wörterbuch zu den Schriften des Neuen Testaments und der übrigen urchristlichen Literatur,</u> 4th revised and augmented ed., 1952. Chicago, Ill.: The University of Chicago Press, 1957. Pp. 909.
An exceedingly useful tool. A second English edition is being prepared which will incorporate the additions made by Bauer in his fifth edition (see the preceding entry). Frederick W. Danker has succeeded Arndt, who died in 1957.

1950 ——   See Metzger, <u>Index of ... Festschriften</u> (III, A, 2, above), nos. 937-980, and <u>Supplement,</u> nos. 72-75, with the cross references at the end of each section.

1950 —— 1900   See Bowman, <u>Bibliography</u> (III, A, 1, above), nos. 2,370-2,382.

1945 —— 1940   See the four bibliographies edited separately and jointly by W. N. Lyons and M. M. Parvis (III, A, 1, above). For the period 1940-1942 it is necessary to look up words as subjects in the main classification; the bibliography for 1943-1945 has an index of Greek words.

1931f ——   Kittel, Gerhard (ed.). <u>Theologische Wörterbuch zum Neuen Testament</u>. Stuttgart:Verlag von W. Kohlhammer, 1932—.
Publication of Vol. 1 began in 1932 and ended July, 1933. Since then the project has reached fascicle 2 (May, 1965) of Vol. 8, the final volume. For the English translation see the next entry.

1931f ——   Kittel, Gerhard (ed.). <u>Theological Dictionary of the New Testament</u>. Translated and edited by Geoffrey W. Bromiley. Grand Rapids, Mich.: Wm. B. Eerdmans Publishing Company, 1964—.
Vol. 1 (793 pages) appeared in 1964; Vol. 2 (955 pages), in 1965. The remaining six will be published at intervals of a year or a year and a half. The translation is intentionally rather literal, and the pagination has been held to that of the German original, plus or minus two or three pages. By far the best and fullest bibliographical tool for the study of the NT vocabulary, although the references in the earlier volumes do not, of course, include literature as recent as the later volumes.

40

Comprehensive (Research) Bibliographies

D. SPECIAL SUBJECTS OR AREAS

Encyclopedias and Bible dictionaries constitute collections of bibliographical material arranged by subjects. The best in this respect are listed below. Their main value is that they indicate the standard works on a subject. In all but the most recent, the references are inevitably to older works.

1961 — The Interpreter's Dictionary of the Bible. Edited by George Arthur Buttrick, et al. 4 vols. Nashville: Abingdon Press, 1962.

1956f — Die Religion in Geschichte und Gegenwart. 3. Aufl. herausgegeben von H. v. Campenhausen, et al. 6 Bde. Tübingen: J. C. B. Mohr (Paul Siebeck), 1957-1962.
Special emphasis on bibliography.

1927f — Dictionaire de la Bible: Supplément. Publié sous la direction de Louis Pirot. Paris: Letouzey et Ané, 1928—.
Editorial direction has now passed to H. Cazelles and A. Feuillet. In 1964 the Supplement had reached fascicle 39 (Vol. VII, cah. 25-32) in the P's. A product of Roman Catholic scholarship. In addition to what is expected of a Bible dictionary, this work also contains biographical articles with bibliographies on leading biblical scholars of all faiths.

1925f — Dictionaire de la Bible. Publié par F. Vigoroux. 5 vols. Paris: Letouzey et Ané, 1926-1928.

1915 — Dictionary of the Apostolic Church. Edited by James Hastings. 2 vols. Edinburgh: T. & T. Clark, 1916.

1907f — The New Schaff-Herzog Encyclopedia of Religious Knowledge. Edited by S. M. Jackson, et al. 13 vols. New York: Funk & Wagnalls, 1908-1912.
Baker Book House issued an unchanged reprint in 1949-1950, and later a supplement entitled Twentieth Century Encyclopedia of Religious Knowledge (2 vols.; Grand Rapids, Mich.: Baker Book House, 1955). The NT editor for the latter was Bruce Metzger.

1905f — Dictionary of Christ and the Gospels. Edited by James Hastings. 2 vols. Edinburgh: T. & T. Clark, 1906-1908.

1898f — Encyclopaedia Biblica. Edited by T. K. Cheyne and J. Sutherland Black. 4 vols. New York: Macmillan, 1899-1903.

1897f — Dictionary of the Bible. Edited by James Hastings. 5 vols. Edinburgh: T. & T. Clark, 1898-1904.

1. Intertestamental Judaism; Philo; Josephus

1962 — Marcus, Ralph. "General Bibliography," Appendix C in Josephus with an English Translation ("The Loeb Classical Library"; Cambridge, Mass.: Harvard University Press, 1963), VIII, 567-589.

1954 — Thyen, Hartwig. "Die Probleme der neueren Philo-Forschung," TheolRund, n. F. 23 (1955), 230-246.

1948 — Pfeiffer, Robert H. History of New Testament Times With an Introduction to the Apocrypha (New York: Harper, 1949), pp. 531-541.

1946 — Riesenfeld, Harald. Jésus Transfiguré: L'Arrière-plan de la Transfiguration de Notre-Seigneur ("Acta Seminarii Neotestamentici Upsaliensis," 16; København: Ejnar Munksgaard, 1947), pp. 333-357.

1946 — Marcus, Ralph. "The Future of Intertestamental Studies," in The Study of the Bible Today and Tomorrow, ed. H. R. Willoughby (Chicago, Ill.: The University of Chicago Press, 1947), pp. 190-208.

1946 Rylaarsdam, J. Coert. "Intertestamental Studies since Charles's Apocrypha and
----   Pseudepigrapha," in The Study of the Bible Today and Tomorrow, ed. H. R. Willoughby
1913 (Chicago, Ill.: The University of Chicago Press, 1947), pp. 32-51.

1945 Marcus, Ralph. A Selected Bibliography (1920-1945) of the Jews in the Hellenistic-
----   Roman Period. New York: American Academy for Jewish Research, 1947. [= Proceed-
1920 ings of the American Academy for Jewish Research, 16 (1947), 97-181.]

1942 Marcus, Ralph. "Selected Literature...," Appendices E-M in Josephus with an English
----   Translation ("The Loeb Classical Library"; Cambridge, Mass.: Harvard University
      Press, 1943), VII, 767-782 [see also pp. 783-788].

1937 Goodhart, Howard L., and Goodenough, Erwin R. "A General Bibliography of Philo
----   Judaeus," in Erwin R. Goodenough, The Politics of Philo Judaeus: Practice and Theory
      (New Haven: Yale University Press, 1938), pp. 125-321, 329-348.

1935 Olmstead, A. T. E. "Intertestamental Studies," JournAmOrSoc, 56 (1936), 242-257.
----

2. Hellenistic, Roman Background

1961 Grant, Frederick C. "For Further Reading," appended to Roman Hellenism and the
----   New Testament (New York: Charles Scribner's Sons, 1962), pp. 188-208.
      A classified listing of about 600 books on the background of the NT.

1956 Grant, Frederick C. "Selected Bibliography," in his preface to Edwin Hatch, The In-
----   fluence of Greek Ideas on Christianity ("Harper Torchbooks"; New York: Harper &
      Brothers, 1957), pp. xix-xxxv.
      A classified listing of some 250 books on Greek culture and religion, on Judaism, and
      on early Christian history.

1956 Grant, Robert M. The Letter and the Spirit (London: S.P.C.K., 1957), pp. 149-153.

1943f Bultmann, Rudolf. "Zum Thema: Christentum und Antike," TheolRund, n. F. 16 (1944),
----   1-20; 21 (1953), 1-14; 23 (1955/56), 207-229.

3. Jewish, Rabbinic Background

1962 Wilcox, Max. The Semitisms of Acts (Oxford: The Clarendon Press, 1965), pp. 186-189.

1962 Davies, W. D. The Setting of the Sermon on the Mount (Cambridge, Eng.: The University
----   Press, 1964), 481-504.

1961 Gerhardsson, Birger. Memory and Manuscript: Oral Tradition and Written Transmission
----   in Rabbinic Judaism and Early Christianity ("Acta Seminarii Neotestamentici Upsalien-
      sis," 22; Lund: C. W. K. Gleerup, 1961), pp. 337-366.

1957 Smith, Morton. "Aramaic Studies and the Study of the New Testament," JournBibRel,
----   26 (1958), 304-313.

1955 Farmer, William R. Maccabees, Zealots, and Josephus: An Inquiry into Jewish Na-
----   tionalism in the Greco-Roman Period (New York: Columbia University Press, 1956),
      pp. 211-220.

1952 Davies, W. D. Paul and Rabbinic Judaism: Some Elements in Pauline Theology (2d ed.;
----   London: S.P.C.K., 1955), pp. 342-367.

1952 Moule, C. F. D. "'Semitisms': Literature," in his An Idiom Book of New Testament
----   Greek (2d ed.; Cambridge, Eng.: The University Press, 1963), pp. 188-191.

1947 Kahle, Paul. "Das zur Zeit Jesu in Palästina gesprochene Aramäisch," TheolRund, 17
----   (1948/49), 201-216.
1894

1943   Smith, Morton. Tannaitic Parallels to the Gospels ("Journal of Biblical Literature Mon-
——   ograph Series," Vol. VI; Philadelphia, Pa.: Society of Biblical Literature, 1951), pp.
        199-206.

1934   Guignebert, Ch. The Jewish World In the Time of Jesus, translated by S. H. Hooke ("The
——   History of Civilization"; London: Routledge & Kegan Paul, 1939), pp. 263-277.

4. Dead Sea Scrolls; Qumran Community

Cont.   "Bibliographie," in Revue de Qumran. Paris: Société Nouvelle des Éditions Letouzey
——   et Ané. Vol. 1 = 1958/59.
1956   Continues the bibliographies of Burchard, who himself edited the 3rd-5th fascicles.
        Since Vol. 2, no. 3, W. S. LaSor has edited this department. Books and dissertations are
        listed alphabetically by author; the periodical literature is arranged alphabetically by the
        name of the journal. Indexed annually by subject and author in the main index of the
        RevQum.

1962   Burchard, Christoph. Bibliographie zu den Handschriften vom Toten Meer. 2 Bde.
——   ("Beihefte zur Zeitschrift für die alttestamentliche Wissenschaft," 76, 89.) Berlin:
1948   A. Töpelmann, 1957, 1965.
            The first volume (1,556 items) covers the period 1948-1955; the second (2,903 items),
        1956-1962. Arranged alphabetically by authors. Appendices index translations and com-
        mentary on the individual manuscripts.

1962   Bardtke, Hans. "Qumran und seine Funde," TheolRund, n. F. 29 (1963), 261-292; 30
——   (1964), 281-315.

1960   Betz, Otto. "Qumran und das Neue Testament: Auswahl aus der neueren Literatur,"
——   NTStud, 7 (1960/61), 361-363.
1958

1959   Braun, Herbert. "Qumran und das Neue Testament: Ein Bericht über 10 Jahre
——   Forschung (1950-1959)," TheolRund, n. F. 28 (1962), 97-234; 29 (1963), 142-176, 189-
1950   260; 30 (1964), 1-38, 89-137.
            Arranged as bibliographical annotations to the text of the NT. Part 1 = Mt.-Jn.;
        part 2 = Acts; part 3 = Rom.-Phlm; part 4 = Heb.; part 5 = Jas-Rev. Braun plans a
        book of which this bibliography will be the first section. He plans to add bibliographies
        on theological themes, on the whole relationship of the DSS community to the early
        church, and on methodology and hermeneutics.

1957   Lasor, William Sanford. Bibliography of the Dead Sea Scrolls, 1948-1957. ("Fuller
——   Theological Seminary Bibliographical Series," No. 2.) Pasadena, Cal.: Library of the
1948   Fuller Theological Seminary, 1959. Pp. 92.
            Contains 3,982 items arranged by subjects. Index of authors.

1954   Schmitt, Joseph. "Les Écrits du Nouveau Testament et les Textes de Qumrân: Bilan de
——   Cinq Années de Recherches," RevSciRel, 29 (1955), 381-401; 30 (1956), 55-75, 261-282.
1950

1949   Baumgartner, Walter. "Der palästinische Handschriftenfund," TheolRund, n. F. 17
——   (1948/49), 329-346; 19 (1951), 97-154.
1947

1947   Wagner, Siegfried. Die Essener in der wissenschaftlichen Diskussion vom Ausgang des
——   18. bis zum Beginn des 20. Jahrhunderts: Eine wissenschaftsgeschichtliche Studie.
1780   ("Beihefte zur Zeitschrift für die Alttestamentliche Wissenschaft," 79.) Berlin:
        A. Töpelmann, 1960. Pp. 284. [Bibliography, pp. 248-281.]

5. History of Religions

Cont.   International Bibliography of the History of Religions/Bibliographie Internationale de
——   l'Histoire des Religions. Published [annually] in connection with Numen with the sup-

| 1952 | port of UNESCO and under the auspices of the International Council for Philosophy and Humanistic Studies by the International Association for the Study of the History of Religions. Leiden: E. J. Brill. Vol. 1 = 1952. |

1960 — 1961
Colpe, C. Die religionsgeschichtliche Schule. Göttingen: Vandenhoeck und Ruprecht, 1961. Pp. 265.

1931 —
Bultmann, Rudolf. "Urchristentum und Religionsgeschichte," TheolRund, n. F. 4 (1932), 1-21.

1928 — 1924
Paust, Albert. Allgemeine Religionsgeschichte und Theologie: Sonder-Abdruck aus Jahresberichte des Literarischen Zentralblattes, Jahrgang 1 [-5], 1924 [-1928]. Leipzig: Verlag des Börsenvereins der Deutschen Buchhandler zu Leipzig, 1925-1929. 5 Bde.

1923 — 1914
Religionsgeschichtliche Bibliographie im Anschluss an das Archiv für Religionswissenschaft. Herausgegeben von Carl Clemen. 5 Bde. Leipzig: B. G. Teubner, 1917-1925.

1917 — 1906
Gruppe, Otto. Literatur zur Religionsgeschichte und antiken Mythologie aus den Jahren 1906-1917. Leipzig: O. R. Reisland, 1921. Pp. 448.

1911 —
Bousset, Wilhelm. "Die Religionsgeschichte und das neue Testament," TheolRund, 7 (1904), 265-277, 311-318, 353-365; 15 (1912), 251-278.

1909 —
Jordan, Louis H. "The History of Religions, and its Introduction into the German Universities," ExpTimes, 22 (1910/11), 198-201.

6. Archaeology and the New Testament

1961 —
"Bibliography: Biblical Archaeology," RevExp, 59 (1962), 205.

1961 — 1958
Finegan, Jack. "Archaeology (1958-1961)," JournBibRel, 29 (1961), 317-328.

1958 —
Dinkler, Erich. "Die Petrus-Rom-Frage," TheolRund, n. F. 25 (1959), 189-230, 289-335; 27 (1961), 33-64.

1953 — 1938
Dinkler, Erich. "Literaturbericht zur Christlichen Archäologie 1938-1953," TheolRund, n. F. 21 (1953), 318-340.

1950 — 1901
Wolf, C. Umhau. "Fifty Years of Biblical Archaeology," LuthQuart, 3 (1951), 289-307, 402-411.

1937 —
Hyatt, J. P. "Bibliography of Important Books and Articles on Biblical Archaeology," JournBibRel, 6 (1938), 144-145, 172-174.

7. Geography

1956 —
Baly, Denis. The Geography of the Bible: A Study in Historical Geography (New York: Harper, 1957), pp. 273-282.

8. Text Criticism

1964 — 1962
Duplacy, Jean. "Bulletin de Critique Textuelle du Nouveau Testament, II," RechSciRel, 53 (1965), 257-284 [to be continued].

1962 —
Metzger, Bruce M. The Text of the New Testament: Its Transmission, Corruption, and Restoration (Oxford: The Clarendon Press, 1964), pp. 257-259.

1961   Oliver, Harold H. "Research Survey: Present Trends in the Textual Criticism of the
——   New Testament," JournBibRel, 30 (1962), 308-320.

1961   Duplacy, Jean. "Bulletin de Critique Textuelle du Nouveau Testament: I," RechSciRel,
——   50 (1962), 242-263, 564-598; 51 (1963), 432-462.
1957

1960   Greenlee, J. Harold. Introduction to New Testament Textual Criticism (Grand Rapids,
——   Mich.: W. B. Eerdmans, 1964), pp. 151-154.

1956   Duplacy, Jean. Où en est la Critique Textuelle du Nouveau Testament? Paris: Librairie
——   Lecoffre, J. Gabalda, 1959. Pp. 103. [= RechSciRel, 45 (1957), 419-441; 46 (1958), 270-
1952   313, 431-462, revised.]

1953   Vööbus, Arthur. Early Versions of the New Testament: Manuscript Studies ("Papers of
——   the Estonian Theological Society in Exile," 6; Stockholm: Estonian Theological Society
        in Exile, 1954), pp. 317-348.

1952   Massaux, E. "État Présent de la Critique Textuelle du Nouveau Testament," NouvRev-
——   Théol, 75 (1953), 703-726.
1940

1939   Metzger, Bruce M. An Annotated Bibliography of the Textual Criticism of the New Tes-
——   tament, 1914-1939. ("Studies and Documents," ed. S. Lake and C. Høeg, No. 16) Copen-
1914   hagen: E. Munksgaard, 1955. Pp. 133.
            An exhaustive listing of 1,189 items. Articles on specific NT passages are arranged
        by book, pp. 103-115. Index of authors.

1937   Kümmel, W. Georg. "Textkritik und Textgeschichte des Neuen Testaments 1914-1937,"
——   TheolRund, n. F. 10 (1938), 206-221, 292-327; 11 (1939), 84-107.
1914

1937   Kenyon, F. G. "After Fifty Years: II. The Text of the Greek New Testament," Exp-
——   Times, 50 (1938/39), 68-71.
1888

1933   Vaganay, Léon. An Introduction to the Textual Criticism of the New Testament, trans-
——   lated by B. V. Miller (London: Sands & Co., 1937), pp. 206-208.

1931   Kenyon, Frederic G. Recent Developments in the Textual Criticism of the Greek Bible.
——   ("Schweich Lectures on Biblical Archaeology, 1932") London: British Academy, 1933.

1924   Robertson, Archibald T. An Introduction to the Textual Criticism of the New Testament
——   (New York: George H. Doran, 1925), pp. 265-278.

1913   Prat, Ferdinand. "Bulletin d'Exégèse du Nouveau Testament: Récents Travaux de
——   Critique Textuelle," RechSciRel, 5 (1914), 459-488.

1913   Bousset, Wilhelm. "Der Text des Neuen Testaments," TheolRund, 1 (1897/98), 405-419;
——   4 (1901), 363-380; 6 (1903), 430-437, 471-483; 11 (1908), 378-396; 17 (1914), 143-154,
        187-206.

1913   See the Theologischer Jahresbericht (III, A, 1, above).
——
1881

1898   Vincent, Marvin R. A History of the Textual Criticism of the New Testament. ("New
——   Testament Handbooks," ed. S. Mathews.) New York: Macmillan, 1899. Pp. 185.

9. Philology

Cont.   Bibliographie Linguistique des Annees 1939-47 [cont.]. Publiée par le Comité Inter-
——   national Permanent de Linguistes avec une Subvention de l'UNESCO. Utrecht: Spectrum,
1939   1949—.

Vol. 1 ran 374 pages. Published annually thereafter. The 1962 volume (pub., 1964) contains 9,265 entries.

1960 — Barr, James. The Semantics of Biblical Language (London: Oxford University Press, 1961), pp. 299-303.

1958 — Turner, Nigel. Syntax, Vol. III of A Grammar of New Testament Greek by James Hope Moulton et al. (Edinburgh: T. & T. Clark, 1963), pp. vii-x, and at the beginning of each chapter.

1958 — Turner, Nigel. "Modern Issues in Biblical Studies: Philology in New Testament Studies," ExpTimes, 71 (1959/60), 104-107.

1946 — Wikgren, Allen, with Colwell, Ernest C., and Marcus, Ralph. Hellenistic Greek Texts (Chicago, Ill.: The University of Chicago Press, 1947), pp. ix-xvi.

1938 — Colwell, Ernest Cadman, and Mantey, J. R. (eds.). Hellenistic Greek Reader: Selections from the Koine of the New Testament Period, with Vocabulary and Notes (Chicago, Ill.: The University of Chicago Press, 1939), pp. ix-xv.

1911 — Deissmann, Adolf. "Die Sprache der griechischen Bibel," TheolRund, 1 (1897/98), 463-472; 5 (1902), 58-69; 9 (1906), 210-229; 15 (1912), 339-364.

10. Form Criticism

1961 — Rohde, Joachim. Formgeschichte und Redaktionsgeschichte in der neutestamentlichen Forschung der Gegenwart. 2 Bde. Unpublished dissertation. Berlin, 1962. Pp. 623. [See TheolLitZeit, 90 (1965), 226-228.]

1961 — 1934 Bultmann, Rudolf. "Note to the Torchbook Edition," prefaced to his essay, "The Study of the Synoptic Gospels," in Form Criticism: Two Essays on New Testament Research, translated by Frederick C. Grant ("Harper Torchbooks: The Academy Library"; New York: Harper, 1962), pp. 1-4.

1958 — 1933 Iber, Gerhard. "Neuere Literatur zur Formgeschichte," appended to Martin Dibelius, Die Formgeschichte des Evangeliums, edited by G. Bornkamm (3d ed.; Tübingen: J. C. B. Mohr, 1959), pp. 302-312.

1957 — Léon-Dufour, Xavier. "Bulletin d'Exégèse du Nouveau Testament: Formgeschichte et Redaktionsgeschichte des Évangiles synoptiques," RechSciRel, 46 (1958), 237-269.

1956 — 1929 Iber, Gerhard. "Zur Formgeschichte der Evangelien," TheolRund, n. F. 24 (1957/58), 283-338.

1943 — McGinley, Laurence J. Form-Criticism of the Synoptic Healing Narratives: A Study in the Theories of Martin Dibelius and Rudolf Bultmann (Woodstock, Md.: Woodstock College Press, 1944), pp. 155-162.
A very full bibliography on form criticism through 1943.

1939 — Schick, Eduard. Formgeschichte und Synoptikerexegese: eine kritische Untersuchung über die Möglichkeit und die Grenzen der formgeschichtlichen Methode ("Neutestamentliche Abhandlungen," 18. Bd., 2/3 Hft.; Münster [Westf.]: Aschendorff, 1940), pp. xv-xxiii.

1936 — 1912 Grobel, Kendrick. Formgeschichte und Synoptische Quellenanalyse. ("Forschungen zur Religion und Literatur des Alten und Neuen Testaments," n. F., 35. Hft.) Göttingen: Vandenhoeck & Ruprecht, 1937. Pp. 130.
Pages 67-123 comprise a history of English and American source criticism from 1912-1936 together with a compressed bibliography.

1930 — Dibelius, Martin. "Zur Formgeschichte des Neuen Testaments (ausserhalb der Evangelien)," TheolRund, n. F. 3 (1931), 207-242.

1928   Dibelius, Martin. "Zur Formgeschichte der Evangelien," TheolRund, n. F. 1 (1929),
——   185-216.
1919

11. Synoptic Problem

1962   Farmer, William R. The Synoptic Problem: A Critical Analysis. New York: Mac-
——   millan, 1964. Pp. 308.
         The first five chapters (pp. 1-198) constitute an interpretive history of the problem
       from the author's special point of view. See in addition F. W. Beare's review, JournBib-
       Lit, 84 (1965), 295-297, for omitted items.

1953   Vaganay, Léon. Le Problème Synoptique: Une Hypothèse de Travail ("Bibliothèque de
——   théologie," Ser. III: "Théologie biblique," Vol. 1; Tournai: Desclée, 1954), pp. xiii-xxii.

1953   Léon-Dufour, Xavier. "Bulletin d'Exégèse du Nouveau Testament: Autour de la Question
——   Synoptique," RechSciRel, 42 (1954), 549-584.

1936   See Grobel, Formgeschichte, §10 above.
——
1912

1923   Huby, Joseph. "Bulletin d'Exégèse du Nouveau Testament: Autour de la Question
——   Synoptique," RechSciRel, 14 (1924), 78-94.

12. Life of Jesus and "Quest of the Historical Jesus"

1964   Loos, H. van der. The Miracles of Jesus ("Supplements to Novum Testamentum," Vol.
——   VIII; Leiden: E. J. Brill, 1965), pp. 707-726.

1963   Braaten, Carl E., and Harrisville, Roy A. (trans. and eds.). The Historical Jesus and
——   the Kerygmatic Christ: Essays on the New Quest of the Historical Jesus. (Nashville:
       Abingdon Press, 1964.) Pp. 250.
         An important collection by Bultmann, Stauffer, Conzelmann, Braun, Bartsch, Ott, Van
       Harvey, Schubert Ogden, and the editors. Bibliographical footnotes.

1962   Anderson, Hugh. Jesus and Christian Origins: A Commentary of Modern Viewpoints (New
——   York: Oxford University Press, 1964), pp. 355-360.

1962   Zahrnt, Heinz. The Historical Jesus, translated by J. S. Bowden (London: Collins, 1963),
——   pp. 151-154.

1961   Cobb, John B. "The Post-Bultmannian Trend," JournBibRel, 30 (1962), 3-11.
——
1956

1961   Ogden, Schubert M. "Bultmann and the 'New Quest,'" JournBibRel, 30 (1962), 209-218.
——
1959

1961   Robinson, James M. "The Recent Debate on the 'New Quest,'" JournBibRel, 30 (1962),
——   198-208.
1959

1959   Kümmel, Werner Georg. "Kerygma, Selfhood, or Historical Fact: A Review-Article on
——   the Problem of the Historical Jesus," Encounter, 21 (1960), 232-234.

1959   Barr, A. "More Quests of the Historical Jesus," ScotJournTheol, 13 (1960), 394-409.

1958   Robinson, James M. A New Quest of the Historical Jesus. ("Studies in Biblical Theol-
——   ogy," No. 25.) London: SCM Press, 1959. Pp. 128.
         Survey and comment on the history of the problem, pp. 9-47.

1957   Robinson, James M. "The Quest of the Historical Jesus Today," TheolToday, 15 (1958),
——   183-197.

1956   Barnikol, Ernst. Das Leben Jesu der Heilsgeschichte. Halle (Salle): Veb Max Niemeyer
——   Verlag, 1958. Pp. 567.
        The first half (the "Theologiegeschichtlicher Teil," pp. 21-243) of this massive work is
        a survey of lives of Jesus from the NT period to 1956. Appended (pp. 560-566) is a chro-
        nological bibliography of lives of Jesus from 1920 to 1957.

1956   Biehl, Peter. "Zur Frage nach dem historischen Jesus," TheolRund, n. F. 24 (1957/58),
——   54-76.
1936

1954   Bowman, John Wick. "De Schweitzer à Bultmann," ÉtudThéolRel, 30, 2 (1955), 1-23.
——
1906

1954   Purdy, Alexander C. "Recent Books on Jesus and His Ministry," RelLife, 24 (1954/55),
——   436-442.

1953   Manson, T. W. "The Life of Jesus: Some Tendencies in Present-day Research," in The
——   Background of the New Testament and Its Eschatology, edited by W. D. Davies and David
1911   Daube (Cambridge, Eng.: The University Press, 1954), pp. 211-221.

1952   Piper, Otto A. "Das Problem des Lebens Jesu seit Schweitzer," in Verbum Dei Manet
——   in Aeternum [Festschrift for Otto Schmitz] (Witten [Ruhr]: Luther-Verlag, 1953), pp.
1906   73-93.
        J. M. Robinson cites it as a "long bibliography of American lives of Christ."

1949   Goguel, Maurice. "Histoire des Vies de Jésus," Chapter I of his Jésus (2. éd., entière-
——   ment refondue; Paris: Payot, 1950).
        J. M. Robinson called it "the standard treatment of the quest since Schweitzer." The
        English translation of the first edition (1933) is listed below.

1949   Glasson, T. F. "Jesus and His Gospel, since Schweitzer," ModChurch, 40 (1950), 250-
——   262.
1906

1948   Hunter, A. M. "The Life of Christ in the Twentieth Century," ExpTimes, 61 (1949/50),
——   131-135.
1900

1939   McCown, Chester C. The Search for the Real Jesus: A Century of Historical Study. "In-
——   ternational Library of Christian Knowledge." New York: Charles Scribner's Sons, 1940.
1834   Pp. 338. [Bibliography, pp. 311-320.]

1936   Riddle, Donald W. "Jesus in Modern Research," JournRel, 17 (1937), 170-182.
——

1935   Robertson, J. A. "The Best Books on the Life of Christ," ExpTimes, 48 (1936/37), 65-68.
——

1933   Hoffmann, Jean C. H. Les Vies de Jésus et le Jésus de l'Histoire: Étude de la Valeur
——   Historique des Vies de Jésus de Langue Française, non Catholiques, d'Ernest Renan à
1863   Charles Guignebert ("Acta Seminarii Neotestamentici Upsaliensis," 17; Paris: Prostant
        apud Messageries Évangéliques distributeur, 1947), pp. 221-228.

1933   Cadoux, C. J. "Some Outstanding New Testament Problems: VIII. The Historical Jesus:
——   A Study of Schweitzer and After," ExpTimes, 46 (1934/35), 406-410.
1906

1932   Guignebert, Ch. Jesus, translated by S. H. Hooke ("The History of Civilization"; New
——   York: Alfred A. Knopf, 1935), pp. 539-551.

1932   Macgregor, George H. C. "Recent Gospel Criticism and our Approach to the Life of
——   Jesus," ExpTimes, 45 (1933/34), 198-203, 283-286.

1931   Goguel, Maurice. "The Life of Jesus in Research," Chapter I of his The Life of Jesus,
——   translated by Olive Wyon (London: George Allen & Unwin, 1933), pp. 37-69.
       A second French edition appeared in 1950 (see Goguel, 1949, above).

1929   Windisch, Hans. "Leben und Lehre Jesu," TheolRund, 12 (1909), 145-162, 171-183; 14
——   (1911), 114-137, 199-236; 15 (1912), 110-132, 145-164, 198-210; 16 (1913), 319-341,
1908   386-400, 436-450; 17 (1914), 404-423, 425-446; 18 (1915), 331-349; 19 (1916), 1-21,
       283-293, 353-369; 20 (1917), 18-59, 305-341; n. F. 1 (1929), 266-288; 2 (1930), 207-
       252.

1925   Case, Shirley Jackson. "The Life of Jesus," in Religious Thought in the Last Quarter-
——   century, edited by Gerald B. Smith (Chicago, Ill.: The University of Chicago Press,
1901   1927).

1912   Schweitzer, Albert. Geschichte der Leben-Jesu-Forschung. 2., neu bearb. und verm.
——   Aufl. des Werkes "Von Reimarus zu Wrede." Tübingen: J. C. B. Mohr (Paul Siebeck),
1778   1913.
       Later editions are reprints of this edition. Five chapters are added to the first edition
       to bring the survey down to 1912. The English translation of the first edition (1906) is
       listed below.

1909   Windisch, Hans. "Der geschichtliche Jesus," TheolRund, 13 (1910), 163-182, 199-220.

1907   Hollmann, Georg. "Leben und Lehre Jesu," TheolRund, 7 (1904), 149-171, 197-212, 246-
——   255; 9 (1906), 132-148, 253-275; 11 (1908), 243-257, 265-277.
1902

1906   Sanday, William. The Life of Christ in Recent Research. New York: Oxford University
——   Press, 1907. Pp. 328.
1887

1905   Holtzmann, H. J. "Das leere Grab und die gegenwärtigen Verhandlungen über die Aufer-
——   stehung Jesu," TheolRund, 9 (1906), 79-86, 119-132.

1901   Schweitzer, Albert. The Quest of the Historical Jesus: A Critical Study of Its Progress
——   from Reimarus to Wrede. Translated by W. Montgomery. 3d ed. London: A. & C. Black,
1778   1954. Pp. 410.
       One of the great books of NT research. This survey turned the study of the life of Jesus
       into new channels. A second German edition (1913) is listed above.

1901   Weinel, Heinrich. "Leben Jesu," TheolRund, 5 (1902), 231-245, 278-291.
——
1900

1899   Baldensperger, W. "Leben Jesu," TheolRund, 2 (1899), 59-67; 3 (1900), 9-19, 342-356.

13. Jesus' Teaching: Kingdom of God and Son of Man; Eschatology

1964   Tödt, Heinz Eduard. The Son of Man in the Synoptic Tradition, translated by Dorothea M.
——   Barton (London: SCM Press, 1965), pp. 353-357.

1962   Lundström, Gösta. The Kingdom of God in the Teaching of Jesus: A History of Interpre-
——   tation from the Last Decades of the Nineteenth Century to the Present Day. Translated by
1890   Joan Bulman. Edinburgh: Oliver and Boyd, 1963. Pp. 300. [Bibliography, pp. 279-296.]

1961   Perrin, Norman. The Kingdom of God in the Teaching of Jesus. "The New Testament
——   Library." London: SCM Press, 1963. Pp. 215.
1830   All but the last chapter (i.e., pp. 13-157) consists of a history of this theme in NT schol-
       arship. Bibliography is placed at the beginning of each chapter.

1961   Black, Matthew. "The Son of Man Problem in Recent Research and Debate" ("The Man-
——   son Memorial Lecture," University of Manchester, Nov. 1, 1962), BullJohnRylLib, 45
1957   (1962/63), 305-318.

1958   Héring, Jean. Le Royaume de Dieu et sa Venue: Étude sur l'Espérance de Jésus et de
——   l'Apôtre Paul ("Bibliothèque Théologique"; nouv. éd., rev. et augm.; Neuchâtel:
        Delachaux & Niestlé, 1959), pp. 267-290.

1956   Grässer, Erich. Das Problem der Parusieverzögerung in den synoptischen Evangelien
——   und in der Apostelgeschichte ("Beihefte zur Zeitschrift für neutestamentliche Wissen-
        schaft," Beiheft 22; Berlin: A. Töpelmann, 1957), pp. 224-234.

1953   Beasley-Murray, G. R. Jesus and the Future (London: Macmillan, 1954), pp. 265-276.
——

1864

1949   Wilder, Amos N. Eschatology and Ethics in the Teaching of Jesus (rev. ed.; New York:
——   Harper, 1950), pp. 215-219.

1937   Niven, W. D. "After Fifty Years: VI. Eschatology and the Primitive Church," ExpTimes,
——   50 (1938/39), 325-330.

1888

1936   Bultmann, Rudolf. "Reich Gottes und Menschensohn," TheolRund, n. F. 9 (1937), 1-35.
——

1935   Howard, W. F. "The Best Books on the Kingdom of God," ExpTimes, 48 (1936/37), 393-
——   396.

1933   Flew, R. Newton. "Some Outstanding New Testament Problems: IV. Jesus and the King-
——   dom of God," ExpTimes, 46 (1934/35), 214-218.

1901   Bousset, Wilhelm. "Das Reich Gottes in der Predigt Jesu," TheolRund, 5 (1902), 397-
——   407, 437-449.

1899   Walther, C. Typen des Reich-Gottes-Verständnisses: Studien zur Eschatologie und Ethik
——   im 19. Jahrhundert. München: Kaiser, 1961.

1800

1899   Baldensperger, W. "Die neueste Forschung über den Menschensohn," TheolRund, 3
——   (1900), 201-210, 243-255.

14. Jesus' Teaching: Parables

1960   Linnemann, Eta. Gleichnisse Jesu: Einführung und Auslegung (Göttingen: Vandenhoeck
——   & Ruprecht, 1961), pp. 189-195.

1910

1953   Jeremias, Joachim. The Parables of Jesus, translated by S. H. Hooke (London: SCM
——   Press, 1954), pp. 160-165.

1888   The bibliography is omitted from the revised English edition of 1963. The German edi-
        tions later than that translated above (the 3d) continue the bibliography.

1947   Bonnard, Pierre. "Où en est la question des paraboles évangéliques? De Jülicher (1888)
——   à Jeremias (1947)," VerbCaro, 4 (1950), 81-89.

1888

15. Jesus vs. Paul

1964   Furnish, Victor Paul. "The Jesus-Paul Debate: From Baur to Bultmann," BullJohnRyl-
——   Lib, 47 (1965), 342-381.

1831

1961   Jüngel, Eberhard. Paulus und Jesus: Eine Untersuchung zur Präzisierung der Frage
——   nach dem Ursprung der Christologie ("Hermeneutische Untersuchungen zur Theologie,"
        2; Tübingen: J. C. B. Mohr [Paul Siebeck], 1962), pp. 301-311.

1948   Andrews, Elias. The Meaning of Christ For Paul (Nashville: Abingdon-Cokesbury, 1949),
——   pp. 249-257.

1907   Vischer, Eberhard. "Jesus und Paulus," TheolRund, 8 (1905), 129-143, 173-188; 11
——   (1908), 301-313.

16. Paul: General Survey

1959   Rigaux, Béda. "L'Interprétation du Paulinisme dans l'Exégèse Récente," in Littérature
——   et Théologie Pauliniennes, edited by A. Descamps ("Recherches Bibliques," 5; Paris:
        Desclée de Brouwer, 1960), pp. 17-46.

1957   See Metzger, Index to ... Paul (III, A, 2, above).
——

1956   Donatien, Mollat. "Bulletin de Théologie Paulienne," RechSciRel, 45 (1957), 240-261.
——

1955   Coppens, Joseph. L'État Présent des Études Pauliniennes. ("Analecta Lovaniensia
——   Biblica et Orientalia," Ser. III, Fasc. 3.) Bruges/Paris: Publications Universitaires de
        Louvain; Desclée de Brouwer, 1956. [= EphTheolLov, 32 (1956), 363-372.]

1949   Hunter, A. M. "St. Paul in the Twentieth Century," ExpTimes, 61 (1949/50), 356-360.
——

1900

1949   Kepler, Thomas (comp.). Contemporary Thinking About Paul: An Anthology (Nashville:
——   Abingdon-Cokesbury, 1950), pp. 419-422 [a book list].

1949   Denis, Albert-Marie. "Saint Paul dans la Littérature Récente," EphTheolLov, 26 (1950),
——   383-408.

1937   Cave, Sydney. "After Fifty Years: VIII. The Significance of the Apostle Paul," Exp-
——   Times, 50 (1938/39), 452-456.

1888

1935   Niven, W. D. "The Best Books on St. Paul's Life and Letters," ExpTimes, 48 (1936/37),
——   118-121.

1933   Bultmann, Rudolf. "Neueste Paulusforschung," TheolRund, n. F. 6 (1934), 229-246; 8
——   (1936), 1-22.

1929   Fridrichsen, Anton. SvenskTeolQvart, 6 (1930), 98-109, 274-292.
——

1925

1928   Bultmann, Rudolf. "Zur Geschichte der Paulusforschung," TheolRund, n. F. 1 (1929),
——   26-59.

1845

1928   Schrenk, G. "Neuere Forschungen und Darstellungen zum Verständnis des Paulus,"
——   KirchRefSchweiz, 85 (1929), nos. 1, 2, 4, 7, 11.

1911   Schweitzer, Albert. Paul and His Interpreters: A Critical History. Translated by
——   W. Montgomery. London: A. & C. Black, 1912. Pp. 252.

1641

1916   Vischer, Eberhard. "Paulus im Lichte der neuesten Forschung," SchweizTheolZeit, 34
——   (1917), 1-9, 49-68.

1916   Vischer, Eberhard. "Paulus," TheolRund, 8 (1905), 470-481, 512-532; 13 (1910), 439-
——   453, 462-481; 16 (1913), 247-262, 294-307; 18 (1915), 151-159; 19 (1916), 294-323; 20
1902   (1917), 368-376.

1900   Jülicher, Adolf. "Paulinische Theologie," TheolRund, 4 (1901), 187-198.

1898

1898   Grafe, E. "Paulinische Theologie," TheolRund, 1 (1897/98), 23-30; 2 (1899), 306-316.
——
1896

17. Paul: Life and Chronology

1959   Van Unnik, W. C. Tarsus or Jerusalem: The City of Paul's Youth, translated by George
——   Ogg (London: The Epworth Press, 1962), pp. 73-76.
1894

1918   Windisch, Hans. "Literaturberichten: Neues Testament, I. Zur Chronologie des
——   Paulus," TheolTijd, 53 (1919), 167-176.

1917   Plooij, D. De Chronologie van het Leven van Paulus (Leiden: E. J. Brill, 1918), pp.
——   182-190.

18. Topics in Pauline Theology

1963   Gale, Herbert M. The Use of Analogy in the Letters of Paul (Philadelphia: Westminster,
——   1964), pp. 271-275.

1962   Ljungman, Henrik. Pistis: A Study of its Presuppositions and its Meaning in Pauline Use,
——   translated by W. F. Salisbury (Lund: C. W. K. Gleerup, 1964), pp. 109-115.

1961   Wegenast, Klaus. Das Verständnis der Tradition bei Paulus und in den Deuteropaulinen
——   ("Wissenschaftliche Monographien zum Alten und Neuen Testament," 8. Bd.; Neukirchen
       Kreis Moers: Neukirchener Verlag, 1962), pp. 169-178.

1961   Larsson, Edvin. Christur als Vorbild: Eine Untersuchung zu den paulinischen Tauf- und
——   Eikontexten (Uppsala: C. W. K. Gleerup, 1962), pp. 324-348.

1960   Romaniuk, Kazimierz. L'Amour du Père et du Fils dans la Sotériologie de Saint Paul
——   (Romae: Pontificio Instituto Biblico, 1961), pp. vii-xxii.

1960   Meuzelaar, J. J. Der Leib des Messias: Eine exegetische Studie über den Gedanken vom
——   Leib Christi in Den Paulusbriefen ("Van Gorcum's Theologische Bibliotheek," 35; Assen:
       Van Gorcum, 1961), pp. 175-178.

1960   Neugebauer, Fritz. In Christus: Eine Untersuchung zum Paulinischen Glaubensverständnis
——   (Göttingen: Vandenhoeck & Ruprecht, 1961), pp. 189-196.

1959   Braumann, Georg. Vorpaulinische christliche Taufverkündigung bei Paulus (Stuttgart:
——   W. Kohlhammer, 1962), pp. 83-87.

1958   See Héring, Le Royaume, §13 above.
——

1956   Hamilton, Neill Q. The Holy Spirit and Eschatology in Paul ("Scottish Journal of Theology
——   Occasional Papers," No. 6; Edinburgh: Oliver and Boyd, 1957), pp. 91-94.

1955   Wikenhauser, Alfred. Pauline Mysticism: Christ in the Mystical Teaching of St. Paul,
——   translated by J. Cunningham (New York: Herder and Herder, 1960), pp. 243-246.

1952   See W. D. Davies, Paul, §3 above.
——

1952   Stürmer, Karl. Auferstehung und Erwählung: Die doppelte Ausrichtung der Paulinischen
——   Verkündigung ("Beiträge zur Förderung christlicher Theologie," 2. Reihe, 53. Bd.;
       Gütersloh: C. Bertelsmann, 1953), pp. 193-198.

1940   Tobac, Édouard. Le Problème de Justification dans Saint Paul: Étude de Théologie
——   Biblique ("Universitas Catholica Lovaniensis: Dissertationes . . . ," II, 3; Gembloux:
       Librairie J. Duculot, 1941), pp. xv-xxi.

1913   Knopf, Rudolf. "Paul and Hellenism," AmJournTheol, 18 (1914), 497-520.

19. New Testament Theology or Biblical Theology

1962   Richardson, Alan. "Present Issues in New Testament Theology," ExpTimes, 75 (1963/64),
——   109-113.

1962   Wallace, David H. "Biblical Theology: Past and Future," TheolZeit, 19 (1963), 88-105.

1960   Schnackenburg, Rudolf. New Testament Theology Today. Translated by David Askew.
——   New York: Herder and Herder, 1963. Pp. 133. [The original French edition was Subsidia
        1 of "Studia Neotestamentica."]

1957   Laymon, Charles M. Christ in the New Testament (Nashville: Abingdon Press, 1958), pp.
——   231-242.

1955   Branton, J. R. "Our Present Situation in Biblical Theology," RelLife, 26 (1956/57), 5-18.
——

1954   Gamble, Connolly, Jr. "The Method of Biblical Theology: A Bibliographical Study," In-
——   terpretation, 9 (1955), 91-99.
1940

1953   Hunter, A. M. "Contemporary Religious Trends: New Testament Theology—Where and
——   Whither?" ExpTimes, 66 (1954/55), 269-272.

1953   Dahl, Nils Alstrup. "Die Theologie des Neuen Testaments," TheolRund, n. F. 22 (1954),
——   21-49.

1952   Gamble, Connolly, Jr. "The Literature of Biblical Theology: A Bibliographical Study,"
——   Interpretation, 7 (1953), 466-480.
1930

1951   Davies, W. D. "The Scene in New Testament Theology," JournBibRel, 20 (1952), 231-238.
——

1950f   Bultmann, Rudolf. Theology of the New Testament, translated by Kendrick Grobel (2 vols.;
——   New York: Charles Scribner's Sons, 1951, 1955), I, 357-366; II, 253-260.

1950   Gamble, Connolly, Jr. "The Nature of Biblical Theology: A Bibliographical Study," In-
——   terpretation, 5 (1951), 462-467.
1939

1950   Filson, Floyd V. "New Testament Theology in the Last Decade (1940-1950),"
——   JournBibRel, 19 (1951), 191-196.

1948   Feine, Paul. Theologie des Neuen Testaments. 8. Aufl. bearb. K. Aland. Berlin:
——   Evangelische Verlagsanstalt, 1950. Pp. 451. [Bibliographies at the heads of sections.]

1947   Stauffer, Ethelbert. New Testament Theology. Translated by John Marsh. London:
——   SCM Press, 1955. Pp. 373. [Bibliographies at the heads of sections.]

1946   Love, Julian Price. "Ten Years with Books in Biblical Theology," Interpretation, 1
——   (1947), 379-387.
1937

1915   Bultmann, Rudolf. "Neutestamentliche Theologie," TheolRund, 18 (1915), 264-267; 19
——   (1916), 113-126.
1912

1912   Brückner, M. "Die neuen Darstellungen der neutestamentlichen Theologie," TheolRund,
——   16 (1913), 363-386, 415-436.
1897

1900   Kühl, E. "Biblische Theologie," TheolRund, 1 (1897/98), 248-259; 4 (1901), 227-235.
——

1897

20. Worship and Sacraments

1960 Schnackenburg, Rudolf. Baptism in the Thought of St. Paul: A Study in Pauline Theology,
—— translated by G. R. Beasley-Murray (Oxford: Basil Blackwell, 1964), pp. 209-214.

1960 Beasley-Murray, G. R. Baptism in the New Testament (London: Macmillan, 1962),
—— pp. 396-406.

1959 Jeremias, Joachim. Infant Baptism in the First Four Centuries, translated by David
—— Cairns ("The Library of History and Doctrine"; London: SCM Press, 1960), pp. 101-104.
1658

1958 Warnach, Viktor. "Literaturbericht: Beziehungen der Liturgie zum Neuen Testament,"
—— Archiv für Liturgiewissenschaft, 4 (1955/56), 127-183; 6 (1959/60), 174-255, 483-519.

1958 Jeremias, Joachim. "The Lord's Prayer in Modern Research," ExpTimes, 71 (1959/60),
—— 141-146.

1957 Delling, Gerhard. Worship in the New Testament, translated by Percy Scott (London:
—— Darton, Longman and Todd, 1962), pp. 186-191.

1950 Lampe, G. W. H. The Seal of the Spirit: A Study in the Doctrine of Baptism and Confirma-
—— tion in the New Testament and the Fathers (London: Longmans, Green, 1951), pp. 323-
      328.

1949 Casel, Odo. "Altchristliche Liturgie bis auf Konstantin d. Gr.," Archiv für Liturgiewis-
—— senschaft, 1 (1950), 256-353.

1948 Jeremias, Joachim. The Eucharistic Words of Jesus, translated by Arnold Ehrhardt
—— (Oxford: Basil Blackwell, 1955), pp. 177-183.
1686

1936 Lohmeyer, Ernst. "Vom urchristlichen Abendmahl," TheolRund, n. F. 9 (1937), 168-194,
—— 195-227, 273-312; 10 (1938), 81-99.
1920

21. Early Christian History

1961 Chadwick, Owen. The History of the Church: A Select Bibliography. London: Historical
—— Association, 1962. Pp. 52.

1958 McGuire, Martin R. P. "The History of the Church from Pentecost to 604: A Survey of
—— Research 1954-58," TheolStud, 20 (1959), 82-107.
1954

1953 Kümmel, Werner Georg. "Das Urchristentum," TheolRund, n. F. 14 (1942), 81-95,
—— 155-173; 17 (1948/49), 3-50, 103-141; 18 (1950), 1-53; 22 (1954), 138-170, 191-211.
1933

1945 Baynes, N. H. "Bulletin bibliographique des publications concernant l'histoire du
—— christianisme primitif et de l'ancienne Église, parue en Grande-Bretagne de 1939 a
1939 1945," RevHistRel, 131 (1946), 109-144.

1932 Windisch, Hans. "Urchristentum," TheolRund, n. F. 5 (1933), 186-200, 239-258, 289-301,
—— 319-334.
1900

1931 Linton, Olof. Das Problem der Urkirche in der neueren Forschung: Eine kritische
—— Darstellung. ("Uppsala Universitets Årsskrift," 1932; Teologi, 2.) Uppsala: Almqvist &
      Wiksells, 1932. Pp. 211. [Bibliography, pp. xiv-xxxii.]

1930 Case, Shirley Jackson (ed.). A Bibliographical Guide to the History of Christianity.
—— Chicago, Ill.: The University of Chicago Press, 1931; reprint edition, New York: Peter
      Smith, 1951. Pp. 265.

1928   Juncker, A. "Neuere Forschungen zum urchristlichen Kirchenproblem," NeuKirchZeit,
——   40 (1929), 126-140, 180-213.

1925   Willoughby, Harold R. "The Study of Early Christianity," in Religious Thought in the
——   Last Quarter-century, edited by Gerald B. Smith (Chicago, Ill.: The University of Chicago
1900   Press, 1927).

1916   See Bauer (III, B, 9, above).

1910   Scheel, Otto. "Zur Frage des Urchristentums und Katholizismus," TheolRund, 14 (1911),
——   331-350.
1906

1908   Bauer, Walter. "Das apostolische und nachapostolische Zeitalter," TheolRund, 12
        (1909), 459-469.

1903   See Clemen (III, B, 9, above).

22. Gnosticism and New Testament Studies

1964   "A Composite Bibliography on Gnosticism," McCormick Quarterly, 18, 4 (May, 1965),
——   50-53.

1963   Giversen, Søren. "Nag Hammadi Bibliography 1948-1963," StudTheol, 17 (1963), 139-187.
——
1948

1963   Haenchen, Ernst. "Literatur zum Codex Jung," TheolRund, n. F. 30 (1964), 39-82.
——
1955

1960   Haenchen, Ernst. "Lituratur zum Thomasevangelium," TheolRund, n. F. 27 (1961),
——   147-178, 306-338.
1956

1959   Schulz, Siegfried. "Die Bedeutung neuer Gnosisfunde für die neutestamentliche Wis-
——   senschaft," TheolRund, n. F. 26 (1960/61), 209-266, 301-334.

1959   Jervell, Jacob. Imago Dei: Gen 1,26f im Spätjudentum, in der Gnosis und in den paulini-
——   schen Briefen ("Forschungen zur Religion und Literatur des Alten und Neuen Testa-
        ments," n. F. 58; Göttingen: Vandenhoeck & Ruprecht, 1960), pp. 337-354.

1932   Schlier, Heinrich. "Zur Mandäerfrage," TheolRund, n. F. 5 (1933), 1-34, 69-92.
——

1918   Bousset, Wilhelm. "Die Religion der Mandäer," TheolRund, 20 (1917), 185-205.
——

E. RELATED AREAS OF STUDY

1. Classical Antiquity

Cont.   Paulys Realencyclopädie der classischen Altertumswissenschaft. Neue Bearbeitung
——   begonnen von Georg Wissowa, fortgeführt von Wilhelm Kroll und Karl Mittelhaus. Stutt-
        gart: J. B. Metzlersche Verlagsbuchhandlung, 1893—. Supplementbände, 1903—.
            The standard classical encyclopaedia. It is being published in two series. The first
        series began with "A" as above. Then in 1914 the second series began with "R." The
        first series reached "Quosenus" in 1963 (halbband 47); the second, "Vulca" in 1961
        (halbband A17). The Supplementbände, published at irregular intervals, bring the articles
        in the volumes already published up to date.

Cont.   "Bibliographische Beilage," in Gnomon: Kritische Zeitschrift für die gesamte klassische
——   Altertumswissenschaft. Berlin: Weidmann, 1925——. Vol. 37 = 1965.
1924   Published every two months. The "Beilage" in Vol. 63 consists of 80 double-columned
pages. See in particular the headings, "Antike Autoren: Biblia, Test. Nov."; "Philologie";
"Religion"; "Grammatik, Lexica"; "Paläographie."

Cont.   Marouzeau, Jules (ed.). L'Année Philologique: Bibliographie critique et analytique de
——   l'antiquité gréco-latine. Paris: Société d'édition "Les Belles Lettres," 1928——.
1924   Published annually. The 1928 volume covered 1924-1926.

1954   Rounds, Dorothy. Articles on Antiquity in Festschriften: The Ancient Near East, Old
——   Testament, Greece, Rome, Roman Law, Byzantium. Cambridge, Mass.: Harvard University Press, 1962. Pp. 560.
     Designed not to overlap Metzger's Index (III, A, 2, above). Contains 35,000 entries
from 1,178 volumes.

1952   Nairn, J. A. Classical Hand-List. 3d ed., rev. and enlarged. Oxford: B. H. Blackwell,
——   1953. Pp. 164.
     A list of standard editions of Classical authors and of secondary works on the Classical
period. Index of authors.

1952   Riesenfeld, Harald, and Riesenfeld, Blenda (eds.). Repertorium Lexicographicum
——   Graecum: A Catalogue of Indexes and Dictionaries to Greek Authors. ("Coniectanea
Neotestamentica," No. 14.) Stockholm: Almqvist & Wiksell, 1954. Pp. 95.
     A listing of standard reference tools for Classical and post-Classical Greek authors.

1924   Marouzeau, Jules (ed.). Dix Années de Bibliographie Classique: Bibliographie critique
——   et analytique de l'antiquité gréco-latine pour la période 1914-1924. 2 vols. Paris:
1914   Société d'édition "Les Belles Lettres," 1927-1928.

2. Patristic Studies

Cont.   Bibliographia Patristica: Internationale Patristische Bibliographie. Herausgegeben von
——   W. Schneemelcher. Berlin: Walter de Gruyter, 1959——. Annually. Vol. 1 = 1956.
1956   This fine tool lists over 1,300 items a year. It is classified, has numerous cross references, and is indexed by names (including the names of authors of reviews). Unfortunately,
and probably inevitably, there is a two-year interval between the close of the year under
review and the publication of the annual volume.

Cont.   Revue d'Histoire Ecclésiastique, II. Bibliographie. Louvain: Université Catholique de
——   Louvain, 1900——. Vol. 60 = 1965.
1900   Appears quarterly as the second half of the RevHistEccl, and since Vol. 4 has had a
separate pagination. The classification scheme completes three cycles a year; the fourth
issue is a list of reviews of books already indexed and the index of names. Vol. 59 listed
10,476 items (exclusive of reviews) covering the period from the NT to modern times.
The triple cycle means that many of the items are less than a year old when they are indexed. Vol. 16 (pub. 1923) is the bibliography for 1914-1919.

Cont.   See L'Année Philologique (1924——) and its predecessor, Dix Années de Bibliographie
——   Classique (1914-1924), §1 above. Look under the names of the patristic authors.
1914

Cont.   Bulletin de Théologie ancienne et médiévale. Louvain: Abbaye du Mont César, 1929——.
——   Vol. 9 = 1962-1965.
1928   This bibliography, a supplement to RechThéolAncMéd, abstracts and comments upon
about 700 items each year. It is indexed by authors in each fascicle, and by names and
subjects at the end of each four-year volume.

1962   Burghardt, Walter J. "Current Theology: The Literature of Christian Antiquity,"
——   TheolStud, 24 (1963), 437-463.
1960

1959   Burghardt, Walter J. "The Literature of Christian Antiquity: 1955-1959," TheolStud, 21
——   (1960), 62-91.
1955

1958   Altaner, Berthold. Patrology. Translated by Hilda C. Graef. Freiburg: Herder, 1960.
——   See p. 44 for a bibliography of patristic bibliographies. In revising the 1949 edition of
       his work Altaner added 4,000 items to his comprehensive and compact bibliographies.

1957f Karpp, Heinrich. "Lateinische Patristik," TheolRund, 24 (1957/58), 253-273; 26 (1960),
——   335-354.
1949

1955   Burghardt, Walter J. "The Literature of Christian Antiquity: Current Projects,"
——   TheolStud, 17 (1956), 67-92.

1954   Campenhausen, Hans von. "Griechische Kirchenväter und Verwandtes," TheolRund, 22
——   (1954), 316-354.
1949

1950   See Metzger, Index of ... Festschriften with Supplement (III, A, 2, above).

1949f Quasten, Johannes. Patrology. Westminster, Md.: Newman Press, 1950—. 3 vols. to
——   date.
           The most detailed recent "patrology." The bibliographies are extended in the French
       translations of the first two volumes, Initiation aux Pères de l'Église, Vol. I (1955), and
       Vol. II (1957).

1948   Karpp, Heinrich. "Altchristliche Literaturgeschichte II," TheolRund, n. F. 14 (1942),
——   199-236; 15 (1943), 1-13, 81-104; 17 (1948/49), 156-161.
1906

1947   Karpp, Heinrich. "Darstellungen der alten Kirche," TheolRund, n. F. 17 (1948/49),
——   73-96.
1934

1946   Campenhausen, Hans von. "Die Kirche im Altertum: Eine Literaturübersicht," in
——   Verkündigung und Forschung: Theologischer Jahresbericht 1942-46 (München: Chr.
1942   Kaiser Verlag, 1946 [?]), pp. 221-242.

1942   See the Bibliographisches Beiblatt der TheoLitZeit (III, A, 1, above).

1921

1936   Klostermann, Erich. "Altchristliche Literatur I," TheolRund, n. F. 9 (1937), 313-328.
——
1913

1933   Campenhausen, Hans von. "Neuere Literatur zur alten Kirchengeschichte," TheolRund,
——   n. F. 2 (1930), 308-332; 6 (1934), 1-32.
1919

1930   Krüger, Gustav. "A Decade of Research in Early Christian Literature (1921-1930),"
——   HarvTheolRev, 26 (1933), 173-321.
1921

1920   Soden, Hans von. "Die Erforschung der vornicänischen Kirchengeschichte seit 1914,"
——   ZeitKirchGesch, 39 (1921), 140-166.
1914

1920   Krüger, Gustav. "Literature on Church History," HarvTheolRev, 14 (1921), 283-374; 15
——   (1922), 323-405; 17 (1924), 1-49, 265-295; 18 (1925), 129-185. [German, Austrian, Swiss,
1914   Dutch, and Scandinavian.]
           Compiled by the former editor of the Theologischer Jahresbericht as a partial continua-
       tion.

1914	Ficker, G. "Alte Kirchengeschichte," TheolRund, 5 (1902), 199-206; 8 (1905), 107-122;
————	9 (1906), 313-326; 11 (1908), 105-111, 134-141, 425-438; 14 (1911), 248-258; 16 (1913),
1897	197-209; 19 (1916), 196-204.

1914	Klostermann, Erich. "Altchristliche Literatur," TheolRund, 11 (1908), 154-167; 13
————	(1910), 315-328; 16 (1913), 262-276; 17 (1914), 224-240.
1905	

1913	See the Theologischer Jahresbericht (III, A, 1, above).
————	
1881	

1908	Lietzmann, Hans. "Altchristliche Literatur," TheolRund, 1 (1897/98), 504-517; 3
————	(1900), 19-28, 56-66; 5 (1902), 99-112; 6 (1903), 28-31; 8 (1905), 345-351; 9 (1906), 14-25,
1896	239-253; 12 (1909), 313-317, 340-354.

1901	Holl, Karl. "Altchristliche Literatur," TheolRund, 3 (1900), 311-317; 4 (1901), 329-
————	331.
1898	

1899	Preuschen, Erwin. "Zur alten Krichengeschichte," TheolRund, 3 (1900), 81-90, 125-135.
————	
1897	

1898	Bernoulli, Carl A. "Altchristliche Literatur," TheolRund, 1 (1897/98), 150-158; 2
————	(1899), 411-419.
1897	

3. Coptic Studies

Cont.	Garnot, J. S. F. "Bibliographie analytique des religions de l'Egypte 1939-43,"
————	RevHistRel, 128 (1944), 94-126; and annually (or more frequently) thereafter.
1939	

Cont.	Simon, Jean. "Bibliographie Copte [fasc. 1 = 1940-1948]," Orientalia, n. s. 18 (1949),
————	100-120, 216-246; fasc. 2 [= 1949], 19 (1950), 187-201, 295-327; etc. annually.
1940	

Cont.	Janssen, Jozef M. A. Annual Egyptological Bibliography / Bibliographie Égyptologique
————	Annuelle. Published for the International Association of Egyptologists. Leiden: E. J.
1947	Brill, 1948—.

1949	Kammerer, Winifred (comp.). A Coptic Bibliography. Ann Arbor, Mich.: University of
————	Michigan Press, 1950. Pp. 250. [Cf. this author's article of the same name, Traditio,
	2 (1944), 507-512.]

1949	Doresse, J. "Les études coptes en Égypte depuis 1939," RevHistRel, 137 (1950), 123-127.
————	
1939	

1945	Simon, Jean. "Contribution à la Bibliographie Copte des Années 1940-1945," Bulletin
————	de la Société d'Archéologie Copte, 11 (1945), 187-200.
1940	

| 1939 | O'Leary, De Lacy E. "Bibliography: Christian Egypt (1939)," JournEgyptArch, 26 (1940), |
| | 148-153. |

4. Palestine

Cont.	Kirjath Sepher: Bibliographical Quarterly of the Jewish National and University Library,
————	Jerusalem. Jerusalem: The Hebrew University Press Association, 1925—. Vol. 40 =
1924	1965.

1949   Thomsen, Peter (ed.). Die Palästinaliteratur: Eine internationale Bibliographie in syste-
────   matischer Ordnung mit Autoren- und Sachregister. Berlin: Akademie-Verlag, 1908—.
1878   Vol. 1 = 1895-1904; Vol. 6 (1956) = 1935-1939.
         Thomsen left at his death in 1954 complete mss. for 1878-1894 and for 1940-1949. Two
       thirds of the former has been published by Leohard Rost and Otto Eissfeldt (1957-1958).
       Covers geography, archaeology, history, etc., down to modern times. Vol. 1 (pp. 905)
       contains 12,818 items.

IV. NEW TESTAMENT SCHOLARS: BIOGRAPHIES AND BIBLIOGRAPHIES

A. BIOGRAPHICAL SOURCES

The abbreviations used in §B for the standard biographical reference tools should present no difficulty, although perhaps it might be explained that "Crockf" = Crockford's Clerical Directory (London: Oxford University Press), and that "ClerDir" = The Clerical Directory of the Protestant Episcopal Church (New York: Church Hymnal Corp.). In addition the following sources have been used:

Dictionaire de la Bible and its Supplément (1926—; listed in III, D, above).
    Cited as "DB" and "DBSup."

Ferm, Vergilius (ed.). Contemporary American Theology: Theological Autobiographies. 2 vols.
    New York: Round Table Press, Inc., 1932-1933.
      Includes "principal publications" with each biography. Cited below as "Ferm, Autobiog."

Howard, Wilbert Francis. The Romance of New Testament Scholarship (1949; listed in II, A, above).
    Cited as "Howard, Romance."

Kepler, Thomas S. (ed.). Contemporary Thinking About Jesus: An Anthology.
    Nashville: Abingdon-Cokesbury Press, 1944.
      Includes brief biographies of the contributors. Cited below as "Kepler, Jesus."

Kepler, Thomas S. (ed.). Contemporary Thinking About Paul: An Anthology.
    Nashville: Abingdon-Cokesbury Press, 1950.
      Includes brief biographies of the contributors. Cited below as "Kepler, Paul."

Kümmel, Werner Georg. Das Neue Testament (1958; listed in II, A, above).
      Includes brief biographies of the principal figures in the history of New Testament study.
    Cited below as "Kümmel, NT."

Lexicon für Theologie und Kirche. 2. Aufl. Herausgegeben von J. Höfer und K. Rahner.
    Freiburg: Verlag Herder, 1957—.
    Cited as "LexThKirch."

The New Schaff-Herzog Encyclopedia of Religious Knowledge (1908-1912; listed in III, D, above).
    Cited as "Schaff-Herzog"; the 1955 supplement as "Sup."

Die Religion in Geschichte und Gegenwart, 3. Aufl. (1957-1962; listed in III, D, above).
    Includes only the most important figures in the history of NT study. Cited as "RGG^3."

Stange, Erich (ed.). Die Religionswissenschaft der Gegenwart in Selbstdarstellungen. 5 Bde.
    Leipzig: F. Meiner, 1925-1929.
      Autobiographical reflections by prominent German scholars. Cited as "Stange, Selbst."

B. INDIVIDUAL SCHOLARS

NOTE: The names of scholars are given in full as the main entry, but on subsequent occurrences abbreviated to initials without periods (except where periods stood in the original).

Aland, Kurt (1915—).
  BIOG.: NTAb, 3 (1958), 103; Wer ist's, '63.

Allo, Ernest-Bernard (1873-1945).
    BIOG.: P. Menoud, "In Mem.," RevThéolPhil, n. s. 33 (1945), 152-154; LexThKirch.

Bacon, Benjamin Wisner (1860-1932).
    BIOG.: Ferm, Autobiog, I, 1-50; Kepler, Jesus, p. 413; Paul, p. 423; Who Was (US);
        DictAmBiog; Schaff-Herzog and Sup; J. Moffatt, "Professor BWB," ExpTimes, 43 (1931/32),
        437-442; "Memorial Resolution," JournBibLit, 52 (1933), iv-v.
    BIBLIOG.: Shirley Jackson Case (ed.), Studies in Early Christianity (New York: The Century
        Co., 1928), pp. 443-457 [1881-1927]; Ferm, Autobiog, I, 49-50 [1927-1931]; B. W. Bacon,
        The Gospel of the Hellenists, edited by Carl H. Kraeling (New York: Henry Holt and Co.,
        1933), pp. 431-432 [1927-1932].

Barnett, Albert Edward (1895-1962?).
    BIOG.: Kepler, Paul, p. 423; NTAb, 3 (1959), 204.

Barr, James (1924—).
    BIOG.: NTAb, 7 (1962), 124; Who's, '65.

Barrett, Charles Kingsley (1917—).
    BIOG.: NTAb, 3 (1959), 320; Who's, '65.

Bauer, Walter (1877-1960).
    BIOG.: Schaff-HerzogSup; Kümmel, NT, p. 561; NTAb, 2 (1958), 287; W. Zimmerli and J.
        Jeremias, "In Memoriam WB," TheolLitZeit, 86 (1961), 313-316; W. Eltester, "Nachruf
        WB," ZeitNTWiss, 52 (1961), v-vi; F. W. Gingrich, NTStud, 9 (1962/63), 1-2 [portrait].
    BIBLIOG.: C.-H. Hunzinger, "Bibliographie WB," TheolLitZeit, 77 (1952), 501-504; cont. in
        RGG[3], I, 925; completed, Hunzinger, TheolLitZeit, 86 (1961), 315-316.
    COMMENT: A. Fridrichsen, Nuntius Sodalicii NT, 7 (1952), 56-60; JournBibLit, 72 (1953),
        xix-xx; F. W. Gingrich, "The Contribution of Professor WB to NT Lexicography," NTStud,
        9 (1962/63), 3-10; W. Schneemelcher, "WB als Kirchenhistoriker," ibid., pp. 11-22; E.
        Fascher, "WB als Kommentator," ibid., pp. 23-38.

Baur, Ferdinand Christian (1792-1860).
    BIOG.: Schaff-Herzog; Howard, Romance, pp. 33-44; Kümmel, NT, p. 561; E. Barnikol, "Der
        Briefwechsel zwischen Strass und Baur: Ein quellenmässiger Beitrag zur Strauss-Baur-
        Forschung," ZeitKirchGesch, 73 (1962), 74-125; RGG[3]; LexThKirch.
    COMMENT: H. Liebing, "FCBs Kritik an Schleiermachers Glaubenslehre," ZeitTheolKirch,
        54 (1957), 225-244; H. Liebing, "Historisch-kritische Theologie: Zum 100. Todestag FCBs
        am 2. Dez. 1960," ZeitTheolKirch, 57 (1960), 302-317; K. Scholder, "FCB als Historiker,"
        EvangTheol, 21 (1961), 435-458; P. Hefner, "Baur versus Ritschl on Early Christianity,"
        ChurchHist, 31 (1962), 259-278; W. Geiger, Spekulation und Kritik: Die Geschichtstheologie
        FCBs ("Forschungen zur Geschichte und Lehre des Protestantismus," 10, 38; München:
        Kaiser, 1964).

Beare, Francis Wright (1902—).
    BIOG.: NTAb, 4 (1960), 299.

Behm, Johannes (1883-1948).
    BIOG.: B. Doehring, "In memoriam JB," TheolLitZeit, 74 (1949), 168-169; LexThKirch.
    BIBLIOG.: TheolLitZeit, 74 (1949), 169-171.

Bengel, Johann Albrecht (1687-1752).
    BIOG.: Schaff-Herzog; Kümmel, NT, p. 561; RGG[3]; LexThKirch.

Best, Ernest (1917—).
    BIOG.: NTAb, 8 (1963), 141.

Billerbeck, Paul (1853-1932).
    BIOG.: J. Jeremias, TheolBlät, 12 (1933), 33-36; Kümmel, NT, p. 561; LexThKirch.

Black, Matthew (1908—).
    BIOG.: NTAb, 3 (1959), 204; Who's, '65.

Bonnard, Pierre (1911—).
    BIOG.: NTAb, 4 (1959), 91.

Bornkamm, Günther (1905—).
  BIOG.: <u>NTAb</u>, 6 (1961), 133; <u>Wer ist's</u>, '63; R. W. Barbour, "Theologians of our Time: XX. Ernst Käsemann and GB," <u>ExpTimes</u>, 76 (1964/65), 379-383.

Bousset, Wilhelm (1865-1920).
  BIOG.: <u>DBSup</u>; <u>Schaff-Herzog</u> and <u>Sup</u>; Kümmel, <u>NT</u>, p. 561; <u>RGG</u>[3]; <u>LexThKirch</u>.

Branscomb, Bennett Harvie (1894—).
  BIOG.: Kepler, <u>Jesus</u>, p. 414; <u>Paul</u>, pp. 424-425; <u>Who's</u> (US), '65.

Bruce, Frederick Fyvie (1910—).
  BIOG.: <u>NTAb</u>, 4 (1960), 188; <u>Who's</u>, '65.

Bultmann, Rudolf (1884—).
  BIOG.: Kepler, <u>Jesus</u>, p. 414; <u>Schaff-HerzogSup</u>; <u>NTAb</u>, 1 (1957), 158; Kümmel, <u>NT</u>, p. 562; RB, "Milestones in Books," <u>ExpTimes</u>, 70 (1958/59), 125; C. K. Barrett, "Note on Professor B," <u>ibid</u>., pp. 125-126; RB, "Autobiographical Reflections," in <u>Existence and Faith:</u> <u>Shorter Writings of RB</u>, edited by Schubert M. Ogden (New York: Meridian Books, Inc., 1960), pp. 283-288; <u>Wer ist's</u>, '63; <u>RGG</u>[3]; <u>LexThKirch</u>.
  BIBLIOG.: A. Fridrichsen (ed.), <u>Bibliographia Dibeliana atque Bultmanniana</u> ("Coniectanea Neotestamentica," Fasc. 8; Lund: C. W. K. Gleerup, 1944), pp. 23-35; <u>Festschrift RB zum</u> <u>65. Geburtstag Überreicht</u> (Stuttgart: Kohlhammer Verlag, 1949), pp. 241-251; "Veröffentlichungen von RB," <u>TheolRund</u>, n. F. 22 (1954), 3-20; S. M. Ogden, "Works of RB Available in English," in <u>Existence and Faith</u>, pp. 318-320; C. W. Kegley (ed.), <u>The Theology of RB</u> (New York: Harper & Row, 1966), pp. 289-310.
  COMMENT: Günther Bornkamm, "Die Theologie RB in der neueren Diskussion: Zum Problem der Entmythologisierung und Hermeneutik," <u>TheolRund</u>, n. F. 29 (1963), 33-141 [Prefaced by a 14-page bibliography in compressed format. Arranged alphabetically. Covers 1941-1962.]; D. E. Nincham, "Theologians of our Time: XIX. RB," <u>ExpTimes</u>, 76 (1964/65), 300-306.

Burkitt, Francis Crawford (1864-1935).
  BIOG.: A. Souter, et al., "FCB," <u>JournTheolStud</u>, 36 (1935), 225-254; K. Lake, "F.C.B.," <u>JournBibLit</u>, 55 (1936), 17-19; J. F. Bethune-Baker, "FCB," <u>ProceedBritAcad</u>, 22 (1936), 445-484; <u>DictNatBiog</u>; <u>Who Was</u>; <u>LexThKirch</u>.
  BIBLIOG.: <u>JournTheolStud</u>, 36 (1935), 337-346.

Burton, Ernest De Witt (1856-1925).
  BIOG.: T. W. Goodspeed, <u>EDWB: A Biographical Sketch</u> (Chicago, Ill.: The University of Chicago Press, 1926); Harold R. Willoughby (ed.), <u>Christianity in the Modern World:</u> <u>Papers</u> <u>and Addresses by EDWB</u> (Chicago, Ill.: The University of Chicago Press, 1926); <u>Christ-Cent</u> (June 4, 1925); <u>DictAmBiog</u>; <u>Who Was</u> (US); <u>Schaff-HerzogSup</u>.
  BIBLIOG.: Willoughby, <u>Christianity in the Modern World</u>, pp. 185-190.

Cadbury, Henry Joel (1883—).
  BIOG.: Kepler, <u>Paul</u>, p. 425; <u>NTAb</u>, 2 (1958), 195; <u>Who's</u> (US), '65; <u>Schaff-HerzogSup</u>.

Cadoux, Cecil John (1883-1947).
  BIOG.: Kepler, <u>Jesus</u>, p. 415; <u>Who Was</u>; <u>Schaff-HerzogSup</u>.

Carrington, Philip (1892—).
  BIOG.: <u>NTAb</u>, 6 (1962), 407; <u>Crockf</u>.

Case, Shirley Jackson (1872-1947).
  BIOG.: Ferm, <u>Autobiog</u>, I, 107-121; S. V. McCasland, "Memorial Resolution: SJC," <u>JournBibLit</u>, 67 (1948), xvi-xvii; <u>Who Was</u> (US); Kepler, <u>Jesus</u>, p. 415; L. B. Jennings, <u>The Bibliography and Biography of SJC</u> (Chicago, Ill.: The University of Chicago Press, 1949); <u>Schaff-HerzogSup</u>.
  BIBLIOG.: Ferm, <u>Autobiog</u>, I, 121-125; J. T. McNeill, M. Spinka, and H. R. Willoughby (eds.), <u>Environmental Factors in Christian History</u> (Chicago, Ill.: The University of Chicago Press, 1939), pp. 399-407; Jennings, <u>Bibliography SJC</u>; Jennings, <u>JournRel</u>, 29 (1949), 47-58.
  COMMENT: Paul Schubert, "SJC, Historian of Early Christianity: An Appraisal," <u>JournRel</u>, 29 (1949), 30-46.

Casey, Robert Pierce (1897-1959).
  BIOG.: J. N. Birdsall and R. W. Thomson (eds.), Biblical and Patristic Studies in Memory of
    RPC (Freiburg: Herder, 1963), pp. 9-10; Who Was (US).
  BIBLIOG.: Birdsall and Thomson, Studies, pp. 265-269.

Chadwick, Henry (1920—).
  BIOG.: NTAb, 3 (1959), 204; Who's, '65; Crockf.

Charles, Robert Henry (1855-1931).
  BIOG.: F. C. Burkitt, "RHC," ProceedBritAcad, 17 (1931); DictNatBiog; Howard, Romance,
    pp. 105-110; H. D. A. Major, "RHC," ModChurch, 46 (1956), 221-226; LexThKirch.
  COMMENT: Paul R. Woudenberg, Pauline Eschatology in the Writings of RHC and Albert
    Schweitzer (Ph.D. dissert., Boston University, 1959).

Clark, Kenneth Willis (1898—).
  BIOG.: NTAb, 3 (1959), 320; Who's (US), '65.

Colwell, Ernest Cadman (1901—).
  BIOG.: Kepler, Jesus, pp. 415-416; NTAb, 3 (1959), 320-321; Who's (US), '65.

Conzelmann, Hans Georg (1915—).
  BIOG.: NTAb, 4 (1960), 188; Wer ist's, '63.

Craig, Clarence Tucker (1895-1953).
  BIOG.: T. Kepler, "Memorial Resolution: CTC," JournBibLit, 73 (1954), x-xi; Kepler, Paul,
    pp. 425-426; Who Was (US).

Cullmann, Oscar (1902—).
  BIOG.: Schaff-HerzogSup; NTAb, 1 (1957), 158; OC, "An Autobiographical Sketch," Scot-
    JournTheol, 14 (1961), 228-233; J. J. Vincent, "Theologians of our Time: XXI. OC," Exp-
    Times, 77 (1965/66), 4-8.
  BIBLIOG.: Frisque, OC (see below), pp. 262-272; enlarged by Willy Rordorf, "Bibliographia
    Cullmanniana," in Neotestamentica et Patristica: Eine Freundesgabe Herrn Professor Dr.
    OC zu seinem 60. Geburtstag überreicht ("Supplements to Novum Testamentum," No. 6;
    Leiden: E. J. Brill, 1962), pp. ix-xix. [Vincent had the use of an "Ergänzung" prepared by
    M. Neubauer and supplied by OC. Therefore, see Vincent's article noted above for recent
    bibliog.]
  COMMENT: M. Bouttier, "L'Oeuvre d'OC," Foi et Vie, 44 (1946), 819-831; G. Rabeau,
    "Bulletin de théologie protestante allemande," RevSciPhilThéol, 32 (1948), 283-291; E.
    Harsveld, The Theology of OC (Th.D. dissert., Union Theological Seminary, N.Y., 1950);
    K. G. Steck, Die Idee der Heilsgeschichte: Hofmann-Schlatter-C ("Theologische Studien,"
    No. 56; Zollikon-Zürich: EVG-Verlag, 1959); J. Frisque, OC: Une Théologie de l'Histoire
    du Salut ("Cahiers de l'Actualité Religieuse"; Tournai: Éditions Casterman, 1960).

Dahl, Nils (1911—).
  BIOG.: NTAb, 3 (1958), 103.

Dalman, Gustav (1885-1941).
  BIOG.: A. Alt, "GD," Palästinajahrbuch, 37 (1941), 5-18; L. Rost, "GD zum Gedächtnis,"
    ForschFortschr, 17 (1941), 371; M. Noth, "GD," ZeitDeutschPalVer, 65 (1942), 1-5;
    O. Procksch, "GD, Ein Gedächtnisblatt," TheolBlät, 21 (1942), 81-90; Kümmel, NT, p. 563;
    RGG³; LexThKirch.
  BIBLIOG.: K. H. Rengstorf, and W. Müller, "Das Schrifttum GD," Wissenschaftliche Zeit-
    schrift...Greifswald, 4 (1954/55), Gesell. und sprachwissen. Reihe Nr. 3, pp. 209-232.
  COMMENT: H.-W. Hertzberg, "Die Stellung GD in der Palästinawissenschaft," ibid., Nr. 4/5,
    pp. 367-372; Rengstorf, "GDs Bedeutung für die Wissenschaft vom Judentum," ibid., pp.
    373-377.

Daniélou, Jean (1905—).
  BIOG.: NTAB, 3 (1959), 321.

Davies, William David (1911—).
  BIOG.: NTAb, 3 (1958), 103-104; Who's (US), '65.

Debrunner, Albert (1884-1958).
  BIOG.: F. W. Gingrich, "Memorial Resolution: AD," JournBibLit, 78 (1958), viii; W. Winter,
    Language, 34 (1958), 335-336; A. Bloch, Gnomon, 30 (1958), 635 ff.

Deissmann, Gustav Adolf (1866-1937).
  BIOG.: Stange, Selbst, I; W. A. Curtis, "Leaders of Theological Thought: AD," ExpTimes,
    40 (1928/29), 5-10; JournBibLit, 57 (1938), vi; Howard, Romance, pp. 117-128; Kepler,
    Paul, p. 426; Kümmel, NT, p. 563; H. Lietzmann, "AD zum Gedächtnis," ZeitNTWiss, 35
    (1936), 299-309 [= his Kleine Schriften, III ("Texte und Untersuchungen," 74; Berlin:
    Akademie-Verlag, 1962), pp. 316-324]; RGG³; LexThKirch.
  BIBLIOG.: Stange, Selbst, I.

Denney, James (1856-1917).
  BIOG.: DictNatBiog; Who Was.

De Zwaan, Johannis (1883-1957).
  BIOG.: W. C. van Unnik, "In Memoriam Prof. Dr. J. deZ," NedTheolTijd, 12 (1957/58), 316-
    318; W. C. van Unnik and G. H. Boobyer, "In Memoriam JdZ," NTStud, 4 (1957/58), 232-
    235; J. W. Doeve, NovTest, 2 (1958), 164-173; G. Sevenster, KerkT, 9 (1958), 71-72; R. M.
    Grant, "Memorial Resolution: JdZ," JournBibLit, 78 (1959), viii-ix.
  BIBLIOG.: Studia Paulina (Haarlem: Erven F. Bohn, 1953), pp. 235-245.

Dibelius, Martin (1883-1947).
  BIOG.: Paul Schubert, "Memorial Resolution: MD," JournBibLit, 67 (1948), xv-xvi; Kepler,
    Paul, p. 426; Kümmel, NT, p. 564; Schaff-HerzogSup; RGG³; LexThKirch.
  BIBLIOG.: Anton Fridrichsen (ed.), Bibliographia Dibeliana atque Bultmanniana ("Coniec-
    tanea Neotestamentica," Fasc. 8; Lund: C. W. K. Gleerup, 1944), pp. 23-35; continued and
    completed by Kümmel, TheolLitZeit, 74 (1949), 131, n. 1, and RGG³.
  COMMENT: W. F. Howard, LondQuartHolRev, 17 (1948), 161-162; Kümmel, "MD als
    Theologe," TheolLitZeit, 74 (1949), 129-140.

Dobschütz, Ernst von (1870-1934).
  BIOG.: Stange, Selbst, IV [portrait]; E. Klostermann, TheolStudKrit, 106 (1935), 1-8;
    JournBibLit, 54 (1935), vi; O. Eissfelt, Saale-Zeitung (Halle), Oct. 31, 1934 [= his Kleine
    Schriften, II (Tübingen: J. C. B. Mohr [Paul Siebeck], 1963), pp. 61-63]; Kümmel, NT,
    p. 564; LexThKirch.
  BIBLIOG.: Stange, Selbst, IV, 31-32.

Dodd, Charles Harold (1884—).
  BIOG.: Kepler, Paul, p. 426; NTAb, 1 (1957), 158; Kümmel, NT, p. 564; Schaff-HerzogSup;
    RGG³; John A. T. Robinson, "Theologians of our Time: XII. C.H.D.," ExpTimes, 75
    (1963/64), 100-102; Who's, '65.
  BIBLIOG.: W. D. Davies and D. Daube (eds.), The Background of the New Testament and its
    Eschatology (Cambridge, Eng.: The University Press, 1956), pp. xiii-xviii [select]; E. E.
    Wolfzorn, EphTheolLov, 38 (1962), 63-70 [complete].
  COMMENT: T. E. McCollough, The Biblical Theology of C.H.D. (dissert., Southern Baptist
    Seminary, 1955); C. F. Evans, "Dr. D, the NT and Eschatology," Theology, 59 (1956),
    492-498; D. A. Walker, An Analysis of the Theology of CHD (Th.D. dissert., Boston Uni-
    versity, 1957).

Duncan, George Simpson (1884-1965).
  BIOG.: Kepler, Paul, p. 427; Who's, '65.

Dupont, Jacques Jean (1915—).
  BIOG.: NTAb, 3 (1958), 104.

Easton, Burton Scott (1877-1950).
  BIOG.: ClerDir, '50; Who's (US), '51; F. C. Grant, "In Memoriam BSE," AnglTheolRev, 32
    (1950), 89-91; JournBibLit, 70 (1950), xix-xx; F. C. Grant, "The Life and Work of BSE,"
    AnglTheolRev, 35 (1953), 147-161 [= BSE, The Purpose of Acts and Other Papers, ed. F. C.
    Grant (New York: Seabury Press, 1954), pp. 3-29 (portrait)].

BIBLIOG.: J. H. W. Rhys, "The Published Writings of Doctor E," AnglTheolRev, 35 (1953), 161-165.

Eltester, Walther (1899—).
BIOG.: NTAb, 5 (1961), 347; Wer ist's, '63.

Enslin, Morton Scott (1897—).
BIOG.: Kepler, Paul, p. 427; NTAb, 5 (1960), 103; Schaff-HerzogSup; Who's (US), '65.

Farmer, William Reuben (1921—).
BIOG.: NTAb, 7 (1962), 124.

Farrar, Frederic William (1831-1903).
BIOG.: Reginald Farrar, The Life of FWF, sometime dean of Canterbury (London: J. Nisbet & Co., 1904); Schaff-Herzog; DictNatBiog; Who Was.

Fascher, Erich (1897—).
BIOG.: NTAb, 7 (1963), 382-383.

Feine, Paul (1859-1933).
BIOG.: Stange, Selbst, V, 39-84; Schaff-Herzog; Kümmel, NT, p. 565; LexThKirch.
BIBLIOG.: Stange, Selbst.

Filson, Floyd Vivian (1896—).
BIOG.: Kepler, Paul, p. 427; NTAb, 2 (1957), 93; Who's (US), '65.

Foakes-Jackson, Frederick John (1855-1941).
BIOG.: DictNatBiog; Who Was; Schaff-HerzogSup; Kepler, Paul, pp. 427-428; H. D. A. Major, "FJF-J, D.D.," ModChurch, 46 (1956), 329-330.

Fridrichsen, Anton (1888-1953).
BIOG.: J. Coppens, EphTheolLov, 30 (1954), 298-299; W. Bauer, "Zur Erinnerung an AF," ZeitNTWiss, 45 (1954), 123-129; JournBibLit, 73 (1954), xii; J. Héring, RevHistPhilRel, 34 (1954), 190; H. Riesenfeld, "AF," SvenskExÅrs, 18/19 (1955), 6-13.
BIBLIOG.: Uppsala Universitets Matrikel 1937-1950 (Uppsala, 1953), pp. 158-162. [See also Bauer's article above.]

Fuchs, Ernst (1903—).
BIOG.: NTAb, 6 (1962), 257; Wer ist's, '63.
BIBLIOG.: "Bibliographie EF," EvangTheol, 12 (1952/53), 583-584.

Fuller, Reginald Horace (1915—).
BIOG.: NTAb 6 (1962), 257; ClerDir, '65.

Gilmour, Samuel MacLean (1905—).
BIOG.: NTAb, 5 (1960), 103-104.

Goguel, (Henry) Maurice (1880-1955).
BIOG.: J. Héring, "M.G.," RevHistPhilRel, 35 (1955), 261-262; P.-H. Menoud, "MG," Verb-Caro, 9 (1955), 1-8; A. Wikgren, "Memorial Resolution: HMG," JournBibLit, 75 (1956), viii; Kepler, Paul, p. 428; Schaff-HerzogSup; RGG[3]; Kümmel, NT, p. 566; M. Simon, "MG," in MG, The Primitive Church, translated by H. C. Snape (London: George Allen & Unwin, 1964), pp. 7-11; LexThKirch.
BIBLIOG.: H. Riesenfeld (ed.), Bibliographia Gogueliana ("Coniectanea Neotestamentica," Fasc. 10; Lund: C. W. K. Gleerup, 1946); Menoud, VerbCaro, 9 (1955), 7-8 [selective].

Goodenough, Erwin Ramsdell (1893-1965).
BIOG.: NTAb, 2 (1958), 195; Who's (US), '65.

Goodspeed, Edgar Johnson (1871—).
BIOG.: Who's (US), '51; J. H. Cobb and L. B. Jennings, A Biography and Bibliography of EJ.G (Chicago, Ill.: The University of Chicago Press, 1948); Kepler, Paul, pp. 428-429; NTAb, 1 (1957), 237; EJ.G, As I Remember [autobiography] (New York: Harper, 1953); Schaff-HerzogSup; RGG[3].
BIBLIOG.: Cobb and Jennings, Biography and Bibliography.

Grant, Frederick Clifton (1891—).
  BIOG.: Schaff-HerzogSup; NTAb, 1 (1957), 237-238; Who's (US), '65; ClerDir, '65.
  BIBLIOG.: S. E. Johnson (ed.), The Joy of Study (New York: Macmillan, 1951), pp. 149-163.

Grant, Robert McQueen (1917—).
  BIOG.: Schaff-HerzogSup; NTAb, 3 (1959), 205; Who's (US), '65; ClerDir, '65.

Grobel, William Kendrick (1908-1965).
  BIOG.: NTAb, 7 (1963), 254-255.

Grundmann, Walter (1906—).
  BIOG.: NTAb, 5 (1960), 104.

Guignebert, Charles (1867-1939).
  BIOG.: M. Goguel, RevHistPhil, 120 (1939), 212-215; M. Brunot, Annales de l'Université de
    Paris, 14 (1939), 365-380; M. Simon, "CG," RevHist, 188 (1940), 179-182; Kepler, Jesus,
    p. 418; Paul, p. 429; Schaff-Herzog and Sup.
  COMMENT: H. G. Wood, "The Radical French Critics, G and Loisy," HibJourn, 52 (1953/54),
    144-155.

Haenchen, Ernst (1894—).
  BIOG.: NTAb, 5 (1961), 237; Wer ist's, '65.
  BIBLIOG.: U. Eichelberg und V. Lorentzen, "Verzeichnis der Veröffentlichungen von EH," in
    Apophoreta: Festschrift für EH zu seinem 70. Geburtstag (Berlin: A. Töpelmann, 1964),
    pp. 1-6.

Harnack, Adolf von (1851-1930).
  BIOG.: G. D. Henderson, "AvH," ExpTimes, 41 (1929/30), 487-491; H. Lietzmann, "Gedächt-
    nisrede auf AvH," SitzPreussAkWiss, phil.-hist Kl, 1931, pp. xlviii-lvii [= his Kleine
    Schriften, III, pp. 302-315]; Howard, Romance, pp. 44-54; Kepler, Jesus, p. 418; Kümmel,
    NT, p. 567; Agnes von Zahn-Harnack, AvH (Berlin: de Gruyter, 1936; 2d ed., 1951); Schaff-
    HerzogSup; RGG³; LexThKirch.
  BIBLIOG.: M. Christlieb, Harnack-Bibliographie, zum 60. Geburtstage AHs (Leipzig: J. C.
    Hinrichs' sche Buchhandlung, 1912); F. Smend, AvH: Verzeichnis seiner Schriften (Leipzig:
    J. C. Hinrichs, 1927); Smend, AvH: Verzeichnis seiner Schriften 1927-1930 (Leipzig: J. C.
    Hinrichs, 1931) [brings the toal to 1,611!].
  COMMENT: A. C. Cotter, "H," TheolStud, 5 (1944), 24-42; H. Hoffmann, "Christentum und
    Antike bei AvH und Ernst Tröeltsch," in Festschrift Tièche (Bern, 1947), pp. 25-40; R. Bult-
    mann, "Introduction [to the 1950 ed. of Das Wesen des Christentums]," trans. S. Attanasio
    and E. Fischoff, in What is Christianity? trans. T. B. Saunders ("Harper Torchbooks"; New
    York: Harper, 1957), pp. vii-xviii; K. Aland (ed.), "AvH," TheolLitZeit, 76 (1951), 245-250;
    W. Volker, "AvH als Kirchenhistoriker," TheolZeit, 7 (1951), 209-227; K. Aland, K. Elliger,
    and O. Dibelius, AH in memoriam, Reden zum 100. Geburtstag am 7. Mai 1951 (Berlin:
    Evang. Verlangsanstalt, 1951); A. von Zahn-Harnack and Axel von Harnack (eds.), AvH:
    Ausgewählte Reden und Aufsätze, Anlässlich des 100. Geburtstages (Berlin: de Gruyter,
    1951); F. V. Filson, "AvH and his 'What is Christianity?' " Interpretation, 6 (1952), 51-62;
    E. Benz, "AvH zum 100. Geburtstag," JahrAkWissLitMaiz (1952), pp. 207-227; F. Hauck,
    "Briefe Hs an Theodor Zahn," TheolLitZeit, 77 (1952), 497-502; W. Pauck, "The Signifi-
    cance of AvH's Interpretation of Church History," UnSemQuartRev, special issue (Jan.,
    1954), 13-24 [= 13, 3 (Mar., 1958), 31-43]; K. Kupisch, "AvH," TheolViat, 6 (1954/55),
    54-87; W. Dulière, "Pour le 25ᵉ Anniversaire de la Mort de H," Le Flambeau, fasc. 6
    (1955), 628-648; fasc. 3/4 (1956), 288-296; G. W. Glick, AvH as Historian and Theologian
    (dissert., University of Chicago, 1957); Glick, "Nineteenth Century Theological and Cultural
    Influences on AH," ChurchHist, 28 (1959), 157-182; E. Fascher, AvH: Grösse und Grenze
    (Berlin: Evang. Verlags-Anstalt, 1962).

Harris, James Rendel (1852-1941).
  BIOG.: A. Souter, "RH," ExpTimes, 32 (1920/21), 105-106; Who Was; DictNatBiog; C. A.
    Phillips, "RH," ExpTimes, 52 (1940/41), 349-352; E. E. Kellett, "JRH," LondQuartHolRev,
    VI, 10 (1941), 201-204; JournBibLit, 61 (1942), vii-viii; Howard, Romance, pp. 92-105;
    Schaff-HerzogSup; LexThKirch.

Hatch, Edwin (1835-1889).
  BIOG.: DictNatBiog; Kümmel, NT, pp. 567-568.

Hatch, William Henry Paine (1875—).
  BIOG.: Kepler, Paul, p. 429; Schaff-HerzogSup; ClerDir, '65.
  BIBLIOG.: WHPH, "Bibliography of the Writings of WHPH," in Munera Studiosa, ed. Massey
    H. Shepherd, Jr., and S. E. Johnson (Cambridge, Mass.: The Episcopal Theological School,
    1946), pp. 179-182.

Headlam, Arthur Cayley (1862-1947).
  BIOG.: Agnes Headlam-Morley, "ACH: A Biographical Essay," in ACH, The Fourth Gospel
    as History (Oxford: Basil Blackwell, 1948), pp. ix-xli; Crockf; DictNatBiog; Schaff-
    HerzogSup; LexThKirch.

Heinrici, C. F. Georg (1844-1915).
  BIOG.: Wer ist's, 1914; Kümmel, NT, p. 568; RGG^3.

Heitmüller, Wilhelm (1869-1926).
  BIOG.: Wer ist's; Kümmel, NT, p. 568; RGG^3.

Héring, Jean (1890—).
  BIOG.: NTAb, 5 (1960), 104-105.
  BIBLIOG.: C. Hauter, RevHistPhilRel, 37 (1957), 1-4 [portrait].

Higgins, Angus John Brockhurst (1911—).
  BIOG.: NTAb, 6 (1962), 257-258; Crockf.

Hilgenfeld, Adolf (1823-1907).
  BIOG.: Wer ist's; Schaff-Herzog; LexThKirch.
  BIBLIOG.: H. Hilgenfeld, Verzeichnis der von AH verfassten Schriften, zusammengestellt von
    der nt. Abt. des theol. Seminars der Universität Jena (Leipzig: O. R. Reisland, 1906); com-
    pleted, ZeitWissTheol, 50 (1907), 14-24.

Holtzmann, Heinrich Julius (1832-1910).
  BIOG.: Wer ist's; Schaff-Herzog; Kümmel, NT, p. 569; DBSup; RGG^3; LexThKirch.

Hort, Fenton John Anthony (1828-1892).
  BIOG.: A. F. Hort, Life and Letters of FJAH (2 vols.; London: Macmillan, 1896); Schaff-
    Herzog; DictNatBiog; Howard, Romance, pp. 69-73; RGG^3; Kümmel, NT, p. 569; LexTh-
    Kirch.
  BIBLIOG.: A. F. Hort, Life, appendix 3.

Hoskyns, (Sir) Edwyn Clement (1884-1937).
  BIOG.: Crockf; DictNatBiog; Kümmel, NT, p. 569.
  COMMENT: J. O. Cobham, "E.C.H.: The Sunderland Curate," ChurchQuartRev, 158 (1957),
    280-295; R. J. Gutteridge, "Sir EH—Wegbereiter, Brückenbauer, Interpret," KerDog, 10
    (1964), 48-60.

Howard, Wilbert Francis (1880-1952).
  BIOG.: Kepler, Jesus, p. 419; Who Was; Schaff-HerzogSup; W. F. Lofthouse, "Dr. W.F.H,
    F. B. A.: An Appreciation," LondQuartHolRev, VI, 21 (1952), 246-251.

Jeremias, Joachim (1900—).
  BIOG.: Schaff-HerzogSup; NTAb, 2 (1957), 93; Wer ist's, '63; M. Black, "Theologians of our
    Time: II. JJ," ExpTimes, 74 (1962/63), 115-119.

Johnson, Sherman Elbridge (1908—).
  BIOG.: Schaff-HerzogSup; NTAb, 2 (1958), 196; ClerDir.

Jülicher, Adolf (1857-1938).
  BIOG.: Stange, Selbst, IV, 159-200; JournBibLit, 58 (1939), iii-iv; H. von Soden, "Akade-
    mische Gedächtnisvorlesung für A. J," TheolBlät, 18 (1939), 1-12; DBSup; Kümmel, NT, p.
    569; RGG^3; LexThKirch.
  BIBLIOG.: Stange, Selbst.

Käsemann, Ernst (1906—).
  BIOG.: NTAb, 5 (1961), 347; Wer ist's, '63; R. S. Barbour, "Theologians of our Time: XX.
  EK and Günther Bornkamm," ExpTimes, 76 (1964/65), 379-383.

Kennedy, Henry Angus Alexander (1866-1934).
  BIOG.: Kepler, Paul, p. 430; DictNatBiog; Who Was; DBSup.

Kenyon, (Sir) Frederick George (1863-1952).
  BIOG.: E. G. Turner, Gnomon, 24 (1952), 527-528; G. Lindeskog, "In memoriam," SvenskExÅrs,
  17 (1952), 164; T. D. Kendrick, et al., BritMusQuart, 17 (1952), 63-70; K. Clark, "Memorial
  Resolution: FGK," JournBibLit, 72 (1953), xxiii-xxiv; S. H. Hooke, PalExpQuart, 85 (1953),
  6-7; J. M. T. Barton, Scripture, 5 (1953), 110-111; Who Was; Schaff-HerzogSup; LexTheolKirch.

Kepler, Thomas Samuel (1897-1963).
  BIOG.: NTAb, 3 (1959), 205; Who's (US), '63.

Kilpatrick, George Dunbar (1910—).
  BIOG.: NTAb, 4 (1960), 189; Who's, '65; Crockf.

Kittel, Gerhard (1888-1948).
  BIOG.: Schaff-HerzogSup; Kümmel, NT, p. 570; RGG^3; LexThKirch.
  BIBLIOG.: G. Reyher, "Bibliographie GK," TheolLitZeit, 74 (1949), 171-175.
  COMMENT: O. Michel, "Das wissenschaftliche Vermächtnis GKs," DeutschPfarrBlatt, 58
  (1958), 415-417; J. Barr, The Semantics of Biblical Language (London: Oxford University
  Press, 1961), passim.

Klostermann, Erich (1870—).
  BIOG.: Schaff-Herzog; W. Eltester, "EK 90 Jahre," TheolLitZeit, 85 (1960), 311-314.
  BIBLIOG.: W. Völker, ZeitNTWiss, 39 (1940), 231-236; H. Nitschke, TheolLitZeit, 75 (1950),
  123-124; W. Eltester, TheolLitZeit, 85 (1960), 314.

Knox, John (1900—).
  BIOG.: Kepler, Paul, p. 430; Schaff-HerzogSup; NTAb, 2 (1957), 94; D. E. Nineham,
  "Theologians of our Time: VI. JK," ExpTimes, 74 (1962/63), 234-238; Who's (US), '65;
  ClerDir.
  BIBLIOG.: J. C. Hurd, "Bibliography of the Work of JK," Festschr. Knox [in prep.].

Knox, Wilfred Lawrence (1886-1950).
  BIOG.: Kepler, Paul, pp. 430-431; Crockf.; Who Was; DictNatBiog; H. E. Wynn, "A Memoir of
  the Author," in WL.K, Penitence and Forgiveness (London: S.P.C.K., 1953), pp. vii-xi; C. H.
  Dodd, "WLK," ProceedBritAcad, 47 (1961), 263-272 [portrait].

Kümmel, Werner Georg (1906—).
  BIOG.: Schaff-HerzogSup; NTAb, 4 (1959), 91; Wer ist's, '63.

Kundsin, Karl (1883—).
  BIOG.: Kepler, Jesus, p. 419.

Lagrange, [Albert] Marie-Joseph (1855-1938).
  BIOG.: L.-H. Vincent, "Le Père L," RevBib, 47 (1938), 321-354 [portrait]; "Memorial Reso-
  lution: MJL," JournBibLit, 58 (1939), ii-iii; DBSup; Schaff-HerzogSup; Kümmel, NT, p. 571;
  LexThKirch.
  BIBLIOG.: L.-H. Vincent, "Essai d'une Bibliographie sommaire du Père L," in Mémorial
  Lagrange (Paris: J. Gabalda, 1940), pp. 1-11; F. M. Braun, The Work of Père L (see below).
  COMMENT: J. Chaine, et al., L'Oeuvre exégétique et historique du RPL ("Cahiers de la
  nouvelle journée," 28; Paris: Bloud & Gay, 1935); F. M. Braun, The Work of Père L,
  adapted from the French by R. T. A. Murphy (Milwaukee, Wis.: Bruce, 1963); R. T. A.
  Murphy, Père L and the Scriptures (Milwaukee, Wis.: Bruce, 1947); F. J. Schroeder, Père L
  and Biblical Inspiration (Washington, D.C.: Catholic University of America Press, 1954);
  B. M. Ahern, "Père M.J.L," Worship, 36 (1962), 242-248; T. McCarthy, "The Spiritual
  Heritage of Père L," CrossCrown, 15 (1963), 396-407; R. T. A. Murphy, "Père L,"
  BibTod, 1 (1963), 478-483.

Lake, Kirsopp (1872-1946).
BIOG.: Kepler, Paul, p. 431; G. K. Lake, "Biographical Note," in Quantulacumque: Studies Presented to KL by Pupils, Colleagues and Friends, edited by R. P. Casey, Silvia New, and Agnes K. Lake (London: Christophers, 1937), pp. vii ff.; H. J. Cadbury, "Memorial Resolution: KL," JournBibLit, 66 (1947), xvii; Who Was (US); Who Was; H. D. A. Major, "KL," ModChurch, 46 (1956), 330-332; Schaff-HerzogSup; RGG[3]; LexThKirch.

Leaney, Alfred Robert Clare (1909—).
BIOG.: NTAb, 6 (1962), 407-408; Crockf.

Leenhardt, Franz Jehan (1902—).
BIOG.: NTAb, 4 (1960), 190.

Lietzmann, Hans (1875-1942).
BIOG.: Stange, Selbst, II, 77-117 [= HL, Kleine Schriften, III, 331-368]; HL, "Antrittsrede," SitzPreussAkadWiss, 1927, 83-86 [= HL, Kleine Schriften, III, 369-373]; M. Dibelius, "HL," ForschFortschr, 18 (1942), 258-259; G. Rodenwaldt, JahrbDeutschArchäolInst, 1942, 507-512; H. Bornkamm, "HL," ZeitNTWiss, 41 (1942), 1-12; W. Eltester, "Der Beitrag der Geschichte zur Theologie: HLs Lebenswerk," TheolLitZeit, 68 (1943), 1-10; H. Bornkamm, Antike, 19 (1943), 81-85; H. Meylan, "In Memoriam," RevThéolPhil, 32 (1944), 202-206; Kepler, Jesus, p. 420; Paul, p. 431; Schaff-HerzogSup; Kümmel, NT, p. 572; Wer ist's; RGG[3]; LexThKirch.
BIBLIOG.: K. Aland, "Die Schriften HLs," ZeitNTWiss, 41 (1942), 12-33 [revised version = HL, Kleine Schriften, III, 377-405].

Lightfoot, John (1602-1675).
BIOG.: DictNatBiog; Schaff-Herzog; DB; RGG[3]; Kümmel, NT, p. 572; LexThKirch.

Lightfoot, Joseph Barber (1828-1889).
BIOG.: W. Sanday, "Bishop L," Expositor, III, 4 (1886), 13-29; F. J. A. Hort, DictNatBiog; Henry W. Watkins, Bishop L (London: Macmillan, 1894) [reprinted from the QuartRev]; G. R. Eden and F. C. Macdonald (eds.), L of Durham: Memories and Appreciations (Cambridge, Eng.: The University Press, 1932); Schaff-Herzog; RGG[3]; Kümmel, NT, p. 572; LexThKirch.
BIBLIOG.: Watkins, Bishop L, pp. 1-12; Hort, DictNatBiog.
COMMENT: Howard, Romance, pp. 56-69; P. H. Richards, "J.B.L as a Biblical Interpreter," Interpretation, 8 (1954), 50-62; L. W. Barnard, "Bishop L and the Apostolic Fathers," ChurchQuartRev, 161 (1960), 423-435.

Lightfoot, Robert Henry (1883-1953).
BIOG.: Kepler, Jesus, p. 420; L. Hodgson, JournTheolStud, 5 (1954), 1-2; D. E. Nineham, "RHL," in Studies in the Gospels, ed. D. E. Nineham (Oxford: Basil Blackwell, 1957), pp. vi-xvi; Who Was; RGG[3].

Lohmeyer, Ernst (1890-1946).
BIOG.: W. Schmauch (ed.), In Memoriam EL (Stuttgart: Evangelisches Verlagswerk, 1951), pp. 9-18; O. Cullmann, "EL," TheolZeit, 7 (1951), 158-160; F. Lieb, "Zum Tod von EL," TheolZeit, 7 (1951), 238-239; E. Ersking, NuntSodalNT, 5 (1951), 33-36; RGG[3]; Kümmel, NT, p. 572; LexThKirch.
BIBLIOG.: Schmauch, In Memoriam, pp. 368-375.
COMMENT: E. Ersking, Glaube und Geschichte in der theologischen Exegese EL: Zugleich ein Beitrag zur Geschichte der neutestamentlichen Interpretation ("Acta Seminarii Neotestamentici Upsaliensis," 18; Lund: Gleerup, 1951).

Lohse, Eduard (1924—).
BIOG.: NTAb, 6 (1961), 133; Wer ist's.

Loisy, Alfred (1857-1940).
BIOG.: M. Brunot, "AL," RevHist, 191 (1941), 188-189; A. C. Cotter, "AL," TheolStud, 2 (1941), 242-251; M. D. Petre, AL: His Religious Significance (Cambridge, Eng.: The University Press, 1944); J. Guitton, "Souvenirs sur les relations de A.L et de H. Bergson," in Mémorial J. Chaine (Lyon: Facultés Catholiques, 1950), pp. 187-202; A. Houtin and F.

Sartiaux, <u>AL: Sa Vie, Son Oeuvre</u>, edited by É. Poulat (Paris: Éditions du Centre National de la Recherche Scientifique, 1960); F. Heiler, <u>AL: Der Vater des katholischen Modernismus</u> (München: Erasmus-Verlag, 1947); <u>DBSup</u>; <u>Schaff-HerzogSup</u>; <u>RGG</u>^{3}; Kümmel, <u>NT</u>, p. 573; <u>LexThKirch</u>; P. Guérin, "La Vie et l'Oeuvre de L à propos d'un ouvrage récent," <u>RevHistPhilRel</u>, 41 (1961), 334-343; R. Aubert, "Aux Origines de la Réaction Antimoderniste: Deux Documents Inédits," <u>EphTheolLov</u>, 37 (1961), 557-578.
  BIBLIOG.: É. Poulat, in Houtin and Sartiaux, <u>Alfred Loisy</u>, pp. 301-324.
  COMMENT: L. P. Jacks, " 'A Creed in Harmony with Modern Thought,' " HibJourn, 23 (1924/25), 577-587; V. Taylor, "The Alleged Neglect of M. AL," HibJourn, 24 (1925/26), 563-572; L. P. Jacks, "M. L on the Teaching of Jesus," <u>HibJourn</u>, 32 (1933/34), 321-341; L. P. Jacks, "M. L on the Birth of Christianity," <u>HibJourn</u>, 32 (1933/34), 495-513; V. Taylor, "M. L on the Birth of Christianity: A Reply," <u>HibJourn</u>, 33 (1934/35), 22-36; J. M. Lelen, "AL," <u>CathBibQuart</u>, 7 (1945), 96-99; V. Taylor, "L's 'Origins of the New Testament,' " <u>HibJourn</u>, 48 (1949/50), 339-347; L. P. Jacks, "Is L Negligible as a Critic of the New Testament? A Reply to Principal Vincent Taylor," HibJourn, 49 (1950/51), 22-31; J. Coppens, "Le Messianisme Israélite selon AL," <u>EphTheolLov</u>, 27 (1951), 53-69; T. F. Glasson, "L on New Testament Origins," <u>ModChurch</u>, 41 (1951), 317-323; H. G. Wood, "The Radical French Critics, Guignebert and L," <u>HibJourn</u>, 52 (1953/54), 144-155; P. Guérin, "La Pensée Religieuse d'AL," <u>RevHistPhilRelig</u>, 37 (1957), 294-330.

McArthur, Harvey King (1912—).
  BIOG.: <u>NTAb</u>, 7 (1963), 383.

McCown, Chester Charlton (1877-1958).
  BIOG.: Kepler, <u>Jesus</u>, pp. 420-421; <u>Paul</u>, pp. 431-432; W. F. Albright, "CCM in Memoriam," <u>BullAmSchOrRes</u>, 149 (1958), 3-4; J. H. Otwell, "Memorial Resolution: CCM," <u>JournBibLit</u>, 78 (1958), x-xi; <u>IsrExplJourn</u>, 8 (1958), 285.

McGiffert, Arthur Cushman (1861-1923).
  BIOG.: <u>Who Was</u> (US); <u>AlumBullUnionTheolSem</u>, Apr., 1933; "In memoriam ACM," <u>AlumBullUnionTheolSem</u>, Oct., 1933; W. W. Rockwell, <u>ChurchHist</u>, Jun., 1933; <u>HibJourn</u>, Jan., 1934; A. C. McGiffert, Jr., "A Son Looks at His Father's Faith," <u>ChicTheolSemReg</u>, Jan., 1935; <u>DictAmBiog</u>; <u>Schaff-HerzogSup</u>.
  BIBLIOG.: <u>A Bibliography of the Faculty of Political Science of Columbia University, 1880-1930</u> (New York: Columbia University, 1931).

MacGregor, George Hogarth Carnaby (1892-1963).
  BIOG.: Kepler, <u>Jesus</u>, p. 421; <u>Paul</u>, p. 432; <u>NTAb</u>, 6 (1962), 408; <u>Who's</u>, '63; J. Mauchline, "In Memoriam," in <u>The New Testament in Historical and Contemporary Perspective: Essays in Memory of G.H.C.M</u>, edited by H. Anderson and W. Barclay (Oxford: Basil Blackwell, 1965), pp. vii-viii.

Manson, Thomas Walter (1893-1958).
  BIOG.: Kepler, <u>Jesus</u>, p. 422; <u>Schaff-HerzogSup</u>; <u>RGG</u>^{3}; <u>NTAb</u>, 2 (1958), 288; "In Memoriam—T.W.M," <u>NTStud</u>, 5 (1958/59), 87-89; M. Black, <u>ProceedBritAcad</u>, 14 (1949), 325-337 [4 plates]; K. W. Clark, "Memorial Resolution: TWM," <u>JournBibLit</u>, 78 (1959), ix-x; <u>Who Was</u>; A. J. B. Higgins (ed.), <u>New Testament Essays</u> (Manchester: Manchester University Press, 1959), pp. ix-x; H. H. Rowley, "T.W.M: An Appreciation," in <u>Studies in the Gospels and Epistles</u>, ed. M. Black (Manchester: Manchester University Press, 1962), pp. vii-xvi; <u>LexThKirch</u>.
  BIBLIOG.: A. J. B. Higgins (ed.), <u>New Testament Essays</u>, pp. xi-xiv [select].
  COMMENT: C. H. Dodd, "T.W.M and His Rylands Lectures," <u>ExpTimes</u>, 73 (1961/62), 302-303; M. Black, "Theologians of our Time: XIV. TWM," <u>ExpTimes</u>, 75 (1963/64), 208-211.

Masson, Charles (1895—).
  BIOG.: <u>NTAb</u>, 6 (1961), 133-134.

Menoud, Philippe Henri (1905—).
  BIOG.: <u>NTAb</u>, 2 (1958), 288-289.

Metzger, Bruce Manning (1914—).
  BIOG.: <u>Schaff-HerzogSup</u>; <u>NTAb</u>, 1 (1957), 238-239.

Meyer, Heinrich August Wilhelm (1800-1873).
  BIOG.: Schaff-Herzog; Kümmel, NT, p. 573; RGG[3]; LexThKirch.

Michaelis, Wilhelm (1896-1965?).
  BIOG.: NTAb, 4 (1960), 301.

Milligan, George (1860-1934).
  BIOG.: Who Was; DictNatBiog; Howard, Romance, pp. 134-137; Schaff-HerzogSup.

Minear, Paul Sevier (1906—).
  BIOG.: Schaff-HerzogSup; Kepler, Jesus, p. 422; NTAb, 2 (1958), 196-197; Who's (US), '65.

Mitton, Charles Leslie (1907—).
  BIOG.: C.L.M, "Milestones in Books," ExpTimes, 70 (1958/59), 70-74; NTAb, 6 (1961), 134;
  Who's, '65.

Moffatt, James (1870-1944).
  BIOG.: F. C. Grant, "JM," UnRev, 6, 1 (Dec., 1944), 3-4; J. McConnachie, et al., BritWeek,
  116 (1944), 169 ff., 227, 293; E. F. Scott, "JM," RelLife, 14 (1944/45), 23-31; A. J. Gossip,
  "JM," ExpTimes, 56 (1944/45), 14-17; W. S. McCullough, "JM," JournBibLit, 64 (1945),
  xi-xii; Kepler, Jesus, p. 422; Paul, p. 432; Who Was; DictNatBiog; Schaff-HerzogSup;
  RGG[3]; LexThKirch.

Montefiore, Claude Joseph Goldsmid (1858-1938).
  BIOG.: F. C. Burkitt, in Speculum Religionis [Festschr. CGM] (Oxford: The Clarendon Press,
  1929); Who Was; DictNatBiog; JewishEncyc; Kepler, Jesus, p. 423; Kümmel, NT, p. 574;
  RGG[3]; DBSup; LexThKirch.

Montefiore, Hugh (1920—).
  BIOG.: NTAb, 7 (1963), 256; Who's, '65; Crockf, '64.

Moule, Charles Francis Digby (1908—).
  BIOG.: NTAb, 2 (1958), 289; Who's, '65; Crockf, '65.

Moulton, James Hope (1863-1917).
  BIOG.: G. Milligan, "JHM," ExpTimes, 28 (1916/17), 393-396; BullJohnRyLib, 4 (1917), 10-25;
  W. F. Moulton, JHM by his Brother (London: The Epworth Press, 1919); Who Was;
  DictNatBiog; Howard, Romance, pp. 128-134; Schaff-HerzogSup; DBSup; H. K. Moulton,
  JHM, 11th October 1863-7th April 1917 (London: The Epworth Press, 1963).

Moulton, William Fiddian (1835-1895).
  BIOG.: W. Fiddian Moulton, WF.M: A Memoir by His Son (London: Isbister and Co., 1899);
  DictNatBiog.

Munck, Johannes (1904-1965).
  BIOG.: NTAb, 3 (1958), 104.

Nestle, Eberhard (1851-1913).
  BIOG.: Schaff-Herzog; H. Holzinger, WürttNekrol, 1913 (Stuttgart, 1916), pp. 50-79; Erwin
  Nestle, "EN: Zu seinem 100. Geburtstag," Für Arbeit und Besinnung, 5 (1951), 194-198;
  Erwin Nestle, "Aus Briefen von EN," BlättWürttKönGesell, 51 (1951), 143-150; RGG[3];
  DBSup; LexThKirch.
  BIBLIOG.: Holzinger, WürttNekrol.

Nock, Arthur Darby (1902-1963).
  BIOG.: Kepler, Paul, p. 433; Schaff-HerzogSup; RGG[3]; Who's (US), '63; K. Stendahl, Numen,
  10 (1963), 236-237; E. R. Dodds and H. Chadwick, JournRomStud, 53 (1963), 168 ff.; A. J.
  Festugière, RevArchéol, 1 (1963), 203 ff.

Otto, Rudolf (1869-1937).
  BIOG.: Heinrich Frick, Gedächtnisrede für RO, 1937; Kepler, Jesus, p. 423; Paul, pp. 433-434;
  Kümmel, NT, pp. 574-575; Schaff-Herzog and Sup; RGG[3]; LexThKirch.
  BIBLIOG.: Davidson, RO, pp. 207-209; Haubold, Bedeutung [see below].
  COMMENT: F. K. Feigel, "Das Heilige": Kritische Abhandlung über ROs gleichnamiges Buch
  (Haarlem: Bohn, 1929); Th. Siegfried, Grundfragen der Theologie bei RO (Gotha, 1931);

H. Frick, et al., ZeitTheolKirch, 19 (1938), 3-166; W. Haubold, Die Bedeutung der
Religionsgeschichtes für die Theologie ROs (Diss. Marburg, 1940); R. F. Davidson, RO's
Interpretation of Religion (Princeton, N.J.: Princeton University Press, 1947); B. Forell,
H. Frick, and F. Heiler, Religionswissenschaft in neuer Sicht: Drei Reden über ROs
Persönlichkeit und Werk (Marburg: N.G. Elwert Verlag, 1951).

Peake, Arthur Samuel (1865-1929).
   BIOG.: L. S. Peake, ASP: A Memoir (London: Hodder & Stoughton, 1930); Who Was;
   DictNatBiog; RGG^3; DBSup.
   BIBLIOG.: Wilkinson, Essays.
   COMMENT: ASP: Essays in Commemoration, edited by J. T. Wilkinson (London: Epworth
   Press, 1958).

Piper, Otto Alfred (1891—).
   BIOG.: NTAb, 6 (1962), 408; J. I. McCord, "OP: An Appreciation," in Current Issues in New
   Testament Interpretation, ed. W. Klassen and G. F. Snyder (New York: Harper, 1962), pp.
   xi-xiv; Schaff-HerzogSup; Wer ist's, '63; Who's (US), '65.
   BIBLIOG.: Klassen and Snyder, Current Issues, pp. 247-260.

Porter, Frank Chamberlin (1859-1946).
   BIOG.: Ferm, Autobiog, II, 197-242; Schaff-Herzog; M. Burrows, "Memorial Resolution: FCP,"
   JournBibLit, 66 (1947), xvi; Who Was (US).
   BIBLIOG.: Studies in Early Christianity, edited by S. J. Case (New York: Century Co., 1928),
   pp. 440-443; Ferm, Autobiog, II, 241-242.

Purdy, Alexander Converse (1890—).
   BIBLIOG.: Harvey K. McArthur (ed.), New Testament Sidelights (Hartford, Conn.: Hartford
   Seminary Foundation Press, 1960), pp. 129-135.

Ramsay, (Sir) William Mitchell (1851-1939).
   BIOG.: W. F. Howard, Romance, pp. 138-155 [= RelLife, 8 (1939), 580-590]; Who Was;
   DictNatBiog; LexThKirch.
   BIBLIOG.: A. M. Ramsay, "A List of the Published Writings of Sir WMR," in Anatolian
   Studies, edited by W. H. Buckler and W. M. Calder (Manchester: The University Press,
   1923), pp. xiii-xxxviii.

Reicke, Bo Ivar (1914—).
   BIOG.: NTAb, 5 (1961), 237-238.

Reitzenstein, Richard (1861-1931).
   BIOG.: Kümmel, NT, p. 576; RGG^3; LexThKirch.
   BIBLIOG.: Festschrift RR zum 2. April 1931 dargebracht, hrsg. von E. Fraenkel, et al.
   (Leipzig: B. G. Teubner, 1931).

Rigaux, Béda (1899—).
   BIOG.: NTAb, 2 (1958), 289.

Robertson, Archibald Thomas (1863-1934).
   BIOG.: "Memorial Resolution: ATR," JournBibLit, 55 (1936), iv; Schaff-Herzog and Sup;
   Who Was (US); E. Gill, A.T.R: A Biography (New York: Macmillan, 1943).

Robinson, Benjamin Willard (1883-1942).
   BIOG.: Kepler, Jesus, p. 424; Who Was (US).

Robinson, Joseph Armitage (1858-1933).
   BIOG.: Schaff-Herzog; F. C. Burkitt, "Memoir JAR," JournTheolStud, 34 (1933), 225-231;
   J. M. Creed, ProceedBritAcad, 20 (1934), 297-308; Who Was; DictNatBiog; LexThKirch.

Robinson, James McConkey (1924—).
   BIOG.: NTAb, 6 (1961), 134.

Robinson, John Arthur Thomas (1919—).
   BIOG.: NTAb, 3 (1959), 321-322; Who's, '65; Crockf.

Ropes, James Hardy (1866-1933).
 BIOG.: "Memorial Resolution: JHR," JournBibLit, 53 (1934), vii-viii; Who Was (US).

Sanday, William (1843-1920).
 BIOG.: Crockf; F. C. Burkitt, "WS," ExpTimes, 31 (1919/20), 20-21; A. Plummer, "WS and
  his Work," ExpTimes, 32 (1920/21), 151-155, 199-203, 247-252; W. Lock, "WS,"
  JournTheolStud, 22 (1920/21), 97-104; Schaff-Herzog and Sup; Who Was; DictNatBiog; RGG³;
  LexThKirch.
 BIBLIOG.: A. Souter, "A Bibliography of Dr. S," JournTheolStud, 22 (1920/21), 193-205.
 COMMENT: D. M. Baillie, "The Christological Theory of WS," ExpTimes, 64 (1952/53),
  236-239; A. R. Vine, "S's Christological Hypothesis," ExpTimes, 67 (1955/56), 49-52;
  H. D. A. Major, ModChurch, 46 (1956), 326-328.

Sanders, Joseph Newbould (1913-1961).
 BIOG.: NTAb, 3 (1959), 206; Crockf; K. Grayston, "JNS," NTStud, 9 (1962/63), 73-74
  [portrait].

Sandmel, Samuel (1911—).
 BIOG.: NTAb, 2 (1957), 94; Who's (US), '65.

Schmidt, Karl Ludwig (1891-1956).
 BIOG.: Kümmel, NT, p. 577; O. Cullmann, "K.L.S," TheolZeit, 12 (1956), 1-9 [portrait];
  RGG³; LexThKirch.

Schnackenburg, Rudolf (1914—).
 BIOG.: NTAb, 2 (1957), 94-95; Wer ist's, '63.

Schniewind, Julius Daniel (1883-1948).
 BIOG.: G. Bornkamm, "JS zum 65. Geburtstag," TheolLitZeit, 73 (1948), 303-304; O. Michel,
  "In memoriam JS," EvangTheol, 8 (1948/49), 337-343; G. Heinzelmann, "In memoriam
  JS," TheolLitZeit, 74 (1949), 165-166; Kümmel, NT, p. 577; RGG³.
 BIBLIOG.: E. Kähler, "Bibliographie JS," TheolLitZeit, 74 (1949), 166-168.

Schoeps, Hans-Joachim (1909—).
 BIOG.: NTAb, 7 (1963), 383-384; Wer ist's, '63.
 BIBLIOG.: Bibliographie der wissenschaftlichen Publikationen von H-JS bis 1950 (Erlangen:
  Universitätsdruckerei, 1950); ZeitRelGeist, 6 (1954), 95-96 [1949-1953].

Schweitzer, Albert (1875-1965).
 BIOG.: AS, Out of My Life and Thought: An Autobiography, translated by C. T. Campion (New
  York: Holt, Rinehart and Winston, 1949); Schaff-Herzog and Sup; Kepler, Jesus, p. 424;
  Kümmel, NT, p. 578; RGG³; Wer ist's, '63 [see also the bibliographies].
 BIBLIOG.: A. A. Roback, "A Tentative AS Bibliography," in The AS Jubilee Book, edited by
  A. A. Roback, et al. (Cambridge, Mass.: Sci-Art Publishers, 1945), 469-483; R. Amadou,
  AS: Éléments de Biographie et de Bibliographie (Paris: L'Arche, 1952) [882 books and
  articles to mid-1952; classified index]; R. Grabs, AS:Denker aus Christentum (Halle
  [Salle]: Max Niemeyer, 1958), pp. 184-189.
 COMMENT: E. N. Mozley, The Theology of AS for Christian Inquirers (London: A. & C.
  Black, 1950); H. G. Wood, "Important and Influential Foreign Books: AS and Eschatology,"
  ExpTimes, 65 (1953/54), 206-209; H. Schuster, "Die konsequent Eschatologie in der
  Interpretation des Neuen Testaments kritisch betrachtet," ZeitNTWiss, 47 (1956), 1-25;
  W. G. Kümmel, "L'Eschatologie Conséquent d'AS jugée par ses Contemporains,"
  RevHistPhilRel, 37 (1957), 58-70; P. R. Woudenberg, Pauline Eschatology in the Writings
  of R. H. Charles and AS (Ph.D. dissert., Boston University, 1959); AS: Mensch und Werk,
  Eine kleine Festgabe zu seinem 85. Geburtstag, von Willy Bremi, et al. (Bern: P. Haupt,
  1959); F. Buri, ASs Wahrheit in Anfectung und Bewährung (Zürich: Artemis Verlag, 1960);
  H. W. Bähr (ed.), AS, Sein Denken und sein Weg (Tübingen: J. C. B. Mohr, 1962); R. Grabs,
  AS, Dienst am Menschen: Ein Lebensbild (4. Aufl.; Halle [Salle]; Max Niemeyer, 1964).

Schweizer, Eduard (1913—).
 BIOG.: NTAb, 3 (1959), 322; Wer ist's, '63.

Scott, Charles Archibald Anderson (1859-1941).
   BIOG.: Kepler, Paul, p. 436; Who Was.

Scott, Ernest Findlay (1868-1954).
   BIOG.: Ferm, Autobiog, I, 323-336; Schaff-Herzog; Kepler, Jesus, pp. 424-425; Paul, p.
      436; J. Knox, "Memorial Resolution: EFS," JournBibLit, 74 (1955), viii-ix; Who Was
      (US).
   BIBLIOG.: Ferm, Autobiog, I, 336.

Soden, Hans (Freiherr) von (1881-1945).
   BIOG.: Schaff-Herzog; Kümmel, NT, p. 579; G. Bornkamm, "In memoriam: HvS, gest. am
      2. 10. 1945," in Verkündigung und Forschung: Theologischer Jahresbericht 1946/47
      (München: Chr. Kaiser Verlag, 1946/47), pp. 153-155; R. Bultmann, "Vorwort," in HvS,
      Urchristentum und Geschichte (2 Bde.; Tübingen: J. C. B. Mohr [Paul Siebeck], 1951-
      1956), I, v-ix; H. v. Campenhausen, Kirche in der Zeit, 11 (1956), 233-236; RGG^3;
      LexThKirch.

Soden, Hermann (Freiherr) von (1852-1914).
   BIOG.: RGG^3; LexThKirch.
   COMMENT: H. Lietzmann, "H.v.Ss Ausgabe des Neuen Testaments," in his Kleine Schriften,
      II, 220-248 [= ZeitNTWiss, 8 (1907), 34-47, 234-237; 15 (1914), 323-331]; H. C. Hoskier,
      "VS's Text of the New Testament," JournTheolStud, 15 (1914), 307-326; P. W. Schmiedel,
      TheolBlät, 1 (1922), 217-223; A. Pott, TheolBlät, 2 (1923), 64-68.

Spicq, Ceslaus (1901—).
   BIOG.: NTAb, 2 (1958), 289.

Stauffer, Ethelbert (1902—).
   BIOG.: Schaff-HerzogSup; NTAb, 4 (1959), 91; F. Baumgärtel, DeutschPfarrBlatt, 60 (1960),
      245-247; Wer ist's, '63.

Stendahl, Krister (1921—).
   BIOG.: NTAb, 1 (1957), 239; Who's (US).

Strauss, David Friedrich (1808-1874).
   BIOG.: Schaff-Herzog; Kümmel, NT, pp. 579-580; RGG^3; LexThKirch.
   COMMENT: K. Barth, DFS als Theologe (2. Aufl.; Zollikon-Zürich, 1948); J. T. Noonan,
      "Hegel and S: The Dialectic and the Gospels," CathBibQuart, 12 (1950), 136-152; V. A.
      Harvey, "D.F.S' Life of Jesus Revisited," ChurchHist, 30 (1961), 191-211; H. Steusshoff,
      "S, Mythos und Wahrheit der biblischen Geschichte," Altertum, 8 (1962), 185-192.

Streeter, Burnett Hillman (1874-1937).
   BIOG.: "Memorial Resolution: BHS," JournBibLit, 57 (1938), v-vi; J. C. Hardwick, "BHS,"
      ExpTimes, 49 (1937/38), 249-254; A. Thornhill, One Fight More: A Biographical Sketch of
      BHS (London: Frederick Muller, 1943); Kepler, Jesus, p. 425; Paul, p. 436; Who Was;
      DictNatBiog; RGG^3; Schaff-HerzogSup; H. D. A. Major, "BHS," ModChurch, 46 (1956),
      267-269; Kümmel, NT, p. 580; LexThKirch.
   COMMENT: M. S. Hostetler, The Place of B.H.S in the Study of the Synoptic Problem (Un-
      published dissertation, Hartford Seminary Foundation, 1952).

Taylor, Vincent (1887—).
   BIOG.: Kepler, Jesus, p. 425; Paul, p. 437; Schaff-HerzogSup; VT, "Milestones in Books,"
      ExpTimes, 70 (1958/59), 231-233; NTAb, 4 (1959), 92; Who's.
   COMMENT: O. E. Evans, "Theologians of our Time: [XIII.] VT," ExpTimes, 75 (1963/64),
      164-168.

Tischendorf, Lobegott Friedrich Konstantin von (1815-1874).
   BIOG.: C. R. Gregory, "De Tischendorfio: de Vita," in his Prolegomena, Vol. III of C.T,
      Novum Testamentum Graece (Leipzig: J. C. Hinrichs, 1894), pp. 3-6; Schaff-Herzog;
      RGG^3; Kümmel, NT, p. 580.
   BIBLIOG.: Gregory, "De Tischendorfio: de Scriptis," Prolegomena, pp. 7-22.
   COMMENT: Howard, Romance, pp. 84-92; K. Junack, "CT in seiner Bedeutung für die
      neutestamentliche Textkritik," Altertum, 2 (1956), 48-56; E. Lauch, "Nichts gegen T," in

Bekenntnis zur Kirche: Festgabe für Ernst Sommerlath zum 70. Geburtstag (Berlin: Evangelische Verlagsanstalt, 1960), pp. 15-24.

Torrey, Charles Cutler (1863-1956).
  BIOG.: Kepler, Jesus, p. 426; Who's (US), '47; W. F. Albright, "Edward Robinson and CCT," BullAmSchOrRes, 120 (1950), 27-28; Schaff-HerzogSup; RGG³; G. Dahl, "Memorial Resolution: CCT," JournBibLit, 76 (1957), viii-ix.

Trocmé, Étienne (1924—).
  BIOG.: NTAb, 7 (1963), 384.

Turner, Cuthbert Hamilton (1860-1930).
  BIOG.: F. C. Burkitt and W. Lock, "Memoir: CHT," JournTheolStud, 32 (1931), 113-118; Who Was; DictNatBiog.

Unnik, Willem Cornelis van (1910—).
  BIOG.: NTAb, 5 (1961), 348.
  BIBLIOG.: J. C. Hurd, Bibliography of the Work of W.C.vU (mimeographed; Austin, Tex.: Episcopal Theological Seminary of the Southwest, 1964).

Weiss, Bernhard (1827-1918).
  BIOG.: BW, Aus neunzig Lebenjahren 1827-1918, hrsg. von H. Weiss (Leipzig: Koehler & Amelang, 1927); Schaff-Herzog; W. Scheffen (ed.), Zum Gedächtnis von BW, 1918; RGG³; Kümmel, NT, p. 581.
  BIBLIOG.: Scheffen, Gedächtnis; RGG² [select].

Weiss, Johannes (1863-1914).
  BIOG.: R. Bultmann, "JW zum Gedächtnis," TheolBlät, 18 (1939), 242-246 [= preface to JW, Die Predigt Jesu vom Reiche Gottes, hrsg. von F. Hahn (3. Aufl.; Göttingen: Vandenhoeck & Ruprecht, 1964)]; Kepler, Paul, p. 437; Kümmel, NT, p. 581; Schaff-Herzog and Sup; RGG³.
  BIBLIOG.: RGG² [select].
  COMMENT: K. Prümm, "JW als Darsteller und religionsgeschichtlicher Erklärer der paulinischen Botschaft: Ein Beitrag zur Vorgeschichte der Entmythologisierung," Biblica, 40 (1959), 815-836; R. Schäfer, "Das Reich Gottes bei Ritschl und JW," ZeitTheolKirch, 61 (1964), 68-88.

Westcott, Brooke Foss (1825-1901).
  BIOG.: A. Westcott, Life and Letters of BFW (2 vols.; London: Macmillan, 1903); Schaff-Herzog; Who Was; DictNatBiog; Kümmel, NT, p. 583; RGG³.
  BIBLIOG.: A. Westcott, Life, II, 441-448.
  COMMENT: Howard, Romance, pp. 73-83; H. T. Kuist, "BFW," Interpretation, 7 (1953), 442-452; C. K. Barrett, W as Commentator (Cambridge, Eng.: The University Press, 1959).

de Wette, Wilhelm Martin Lebrecht (1780-1849).
  BIOG.: Schaff-Herzog; RGG³; Kümmel, NT, p. 583.
  COMMENT: E. Staehelin, Dewettiana: Forschungen und Texte zu WMLdWs Leben und Werk ("Studien zur Geschichte der Wissenschaften in Basel," 2; Basel: Helbing & Lichtenhahln, 1956); R. Smend, W.M.L.dWs Arbeit zum Alten und Neuen Testament (Basel: Helbing & Lichtenhahn, 1958); R. Smend, "DW und das Verhältnis zwischen historischer Bibelkritik und philosophischem System im 19. Jahrhundert," TheolZeit, 14 (1958), 107-119.

Wettstein, Johann Jakob (1693-1754).
  BIOG.: Schaff-Herzog; C. L. Hulbert-Powell, JJW: An Account of his Life, Work, and Some of his Contemporaries (London: S.P.C.K., 1938); RGG³; Kümmel, NT, p. 583.
  BIBLIOG.: Hulbert-Powell, JJW, pp. 306-311.

Wikenhauser, Alfred (1883-1960).
  BIOG.: A. Vögtle, TheolRev, 49 (1953), 68-69; NTAb, 2 (1958), 197-198; J. Schmid, BibZeit, 5 (1961), 92-93.
  BIBLIOG.: Synoptische Studien: AW zum 70. Geburtstag...dargebracht von Freunden, Kollegen und Schülern (München: K. Zink, 1953), pp. 290-293.

Wikgren, Allen Paul (1906—).
  BIOG.: Schaff-HerzogSup; NTAb, 3 (1959), 206.

Wilder, Amos Niven (1895—).
  BIOG.: Kepler, Jesus, p. 426; Paul, pp. 437-438; Schaff-HerzogSup; NTAb, 1 (1957), 239; Who's
    (US).
  BIBLIOG.: Harold R. Willoughby, "The Bibliography of ANW," HarvDivSchBull, 21 (1955/56),
    151-159.

Willoughby, Harold Rideout (1890—).
  BIOG.: Kepler, Paul, p. 438; Schaff-HerzogSup; Allen Wikgren (ed.), Early Christian Origins
    (Chicago: Quadrangle Books, 1961), pp. 150-151.
  BIBLIOG.: Wikgren, Origins, pp. 152-159.

Wilson, Robert McLachlan (1916—).
  BIOG.: NTAb, 4 (1959), 93.

Windisch, Hans Ludwig (1881-1935).
  BIOG.: Kümmel, NT, p. 583; Wer ist's; RGG^3.
  BIBLIOG.: M. J. Fiedler, TheolLitZeit, 81 (1956), 499-510.
  COMMENT: E. Beijer, "HW und seine Bedeutung für die neutestamentliche Wissenschaft,"
    ZeitNTWiss, 48 (1957), 22-49; [= SvenskExÅrs, 18/19 (1953/54), 109-139]; K. Prümm,
    "Zur Früh- und Spätform der religionsgeschichtlichen Christusdeutung bei HW," Biblica,
    42 (1961), 391-422; 43 (1962), 22-56.

Winter, Paul (? —).
  BIOG.: NTAb, 5 (1961), 238.

Wrede, William (1859-1906).
  BIOG.: Schaff-Herzog and Sup; Wer ist's; Kepler, Paul, p. 438; RGG^3; Kümmel, NT, p. 584.
  BIBLIOG.: Strecker, "WW," pp. 89-91.
  COMMENT: G. Strecker, "WW: Zur 100. Wiederkehr seines Geburtstages," ZeitTheolKirch,
    57 (1960), 67-91.

Zahn, Theodor (1838-1933).
  BIOG.: Stange, Selbst, I, 221 ff.; Wer ist's; Schaff-Herzog and Sup; RGG^3; Kümmel, NT, p.
    584; F. Hauck, "Briefe TZs aus seinem ersten Studienjahr in Basel 1854/55," TheolZeit,
    6 (1950), 261-270; F. Hauck, "Briefe Harnacks an TZ," TheolLitZeit, 77 (1952), 497-502.
  BIBLIOG.: Zahn-Bibliographie: Verzeichnis der literarischen Veröffentlichungen TvZs...
    zusammengestellt und dargebracht von Freunden und Kollegen (Leipzig: A. Deichertsche
    Verlagsbuchhandlung Werner Scholl, 1918); Stange, Selbst; RGG^2.